Heaven's Guide To The Other Side

Heaven's Guide To The Other Side

Enlighten Your Awareness In Recognizing Signs from Loved Ones In Heaven

Vanessa Lynn Squeglia
and Her Teams of Angels

Self-published
Vanessa Lynn Squeglia
www.Heavensguide.com

Designed by: Vanessa Lynn Squeglia
Illustrated by: Karen Burgess

ISBN: 1492213500
ISBN 13: 9781492213505

Dedicated to

God
and
Shane

My sources of
love, inspiration
and
encouragement

Contents

To view clearer pictures of photos and illustrations, please refer to my web site, www.Heavensguide.com

Introduction

I was inspired to write this book through a combination of events, circumstances, and of course, my angels! This book is for anyone who is curious about the afterlife. It is written for anyone seeking or needing spiritual validation and reassurance that our loved ones in Heaven are always around us and always supporting us with unconditional love. If you need encouragement while grieving, I am sure you will find this helpful. Everything I talk about is based solely on my own experiences and inner knowledge. I truly feel blessed to be able to share my stories with all who seek.

This book is a collection of spiritual topics presented in an easy-to-understand format. We are all very different, yet we are spiritually connected to one another. We are on our own unique spiritual journey. Every single one of us is part of a universal God consciousness. By reading this book, you will realize there is a higher plan that is implemented by a higher power. I wish you as much enjoyment in reading this book as I had writing it.

Acknowledgments

I need to acknowledge God. Without God-given gifts, I would be unable to help anyone or any animal in the way that I can. I am grateful to God every day for allowing me to have this existence on this planet.

My son, Shane, who has given me strength beyond anything I could imagine.

Special thanks to my Mom, Joan and my Dad, Nicholas, for supporting me in many ways during the most challenging parts of my life.

And of course, to all my friends who supported me with their encouragement, listening to me and who provided quiet places for me to write.

I thank every person I have encountered from Heaven and the ones I have yet to meet, including the animals.

Special appreciation to all my clients who have come to see me as well as the new ones I look forward to meeting in the future.

I thank you for taking time to read what my thoughts and experiences are about.

I love you all!

Part I – My Story and Preface

Coming Out of the Psychic Closet: About the Author

Welcome to *Heaven's Guide to the Other Side.* Since I always like people to feel comfortable and at ease, I'd like you to get to know me. So, here goes!

I grew up in a typical middle-class American family and was born and raised in Connecticut, which is where I still reside. I'm the oldest of three children. My parents decided to wait six years until having their second child. I was probably enough to handle at the time. My brother came along six years later, with my sister beaming in about two years after that. Mom worked full time when I was small, so I attended day care nearby Dad's job, so we commuted together. He would drop me off and pick me up every day. Dad was also attending college at night, studying engineering.

It was about that same time I had an experience with the "other side" when my grandfather transitioned. That is my first recollection of being able to connect with someone in Heaven.

Always having an interest in anything paranormal or spiritual, I gravitated to girlfriends of similar interests around the ages of eleven to twelve. We would talk about some of our experiences and then started experimenting with the Ouija board. (I do not recommend children "playing" with the Ouija board, but we had fun sharing and seeking the interest of the paranormal). We, (mostly me) were conducting little séances and getting answers. Of course, having no clue what we were doing, we invited a lot of strange energies into my parent's house and very strange things began happening, such as experiencing odd burning and musty smells. But even worse, was the bad luck that descended upon the house. We didn't have a clue what we were attracting using such a board. After those strange experiences, we decided the board wasn't a good thing and never used it again.

Aside from playing around with the Ouija board and dabbling with levitation in the seventh grade, I really didn't share my "gifts" or experiences with anyone. Even a friend of mine who had known me for most of my life, never knew the extent of my abilities. I always listened carefully when others would speak about it but, never shared my experiences. I always felt unique, special, and different. It wasn't until sometime in the year 2000 that I decided to come out of the psychic closet. My angels advised me it was time to go public.

All my schooling was completed in the public system. My 1977 high school class was one of the largest in history. Yet shyness was my forte, unless I was with my immediate circle of friends. I was never in trouble and just kind of did my own thing. Most of the time, I felt almost invisible. If you have similar gifts, this may make sense to you. After graduating from high school, I began a full-time job. At that time, indecision was my middle name as far as what to do with my life. After a job offer presented itself and seemed perfect at the time, it was merely one less decision to make. The opportunity was an entry-level clerical position at a major corporation in New Haven, Connecticut, which set the tone for my working career. It started the path of working for large corporations for years to come.

In the early 1980s, while working full time, I attended a business institute and received a certificate in bookkeeping. I later worked for the finance departments of several large companies where I discovered that I needed more contact with people and decided that the accounting field wasn't for me. One thing led to another and my last "job" was working as a manager in a behavioral health managed care company starting in 1991. I participated in building one of New York City's largest behavioral health-care provider networks in the 1990s. The network included psychiatrists, psychologists, social workers, and hospital psychiatric and substance abuse programs. I was beginning to present managed care programs to some of the major hospitals in New York City. Sometimes it involved working seven days a week and long hours. I was commuting from Orange, Connecticut. Despite the hectic schedule and disorganization of this new venute, I enjoyed it.

In between all of that, I married and divorced in the span of about three years. It was during that time, the love of my life, Shane Patrick was born. I separated from the marriage when Shane was fourteen-months-old and have been a single parent ever since. While it hasn't always been easy, it's given me more pleasure and joy to see this little boy grow to become a man.

Shane and I took a trip to the Bahamas in 1994. We visited Rose Island for a day-long excursion. While eating lunch and leaning on the picnic table, I felt something bite my elbow. I never saw it. By the time I looked for it, it was gone. About two weeks later the venom from the bite took hold of my nervous system and I was barely able to move. After many misdiagnoses and almost five years, I was plucked away from my life as I knew it and pointed in a much different direction, one that I never consciously planned. After much prayer, arguing with insurance companies and trying to get the help I needed through conventional medicine, I prayed for anyone who could help me to please step forward. One by one, they appeared. It took a little longer than I had hoped. I was on a disability from my job in New York for almost five years. But because of that experience, I became aware of and received many different holistic therapies, which all contributed to my return to wellness. This all led to my learning various energy therapies which I use in my practice now.

At one point, I remained at a level of health where I didn't improve or worsen. I was receiving Reiki, therapeutic massage, acupuncture, nutritional support and was starting mild exercise, but still didn't feel quite right. I truly didn't understand most of the treatments I was getting, but I knew everything was helping me to feel better. A woman told me about a Chinese doctor who was coming to Connecticut to present a lecture and demonstration. She felt he could help me, so her son drove us that Friday night to East Haven, Connecticut. I'd say there were at least one hundred people there - many more than I would have expected. His name is Dr. Kam Yuen. His technique was called Chinese Energetic Medicine, now named Yuen Energetics. Dr. Yuen captured everyone's attention immediately with a very brief talk, then invited audience members one by one to come up so he could "work" on them for demonstration purposes. He would ask the person for one symptom he or she was complaining about. Then he would waive his hands around, up and down behind the person's back, never touching him or her. My observation was that all those that he worked on were quite pleased and felt relief from their complaint. I watched Dr. Yuen as though this was crazy. Just before he wrapped up the evening, he asked for one more person to come up to him. The woman sitting next to me, Karen, whom I had never met until that night took my arm and raised it into the air. We developed a friendship from that point and she is the artist who drew the illustrations for this book. It's funny how things work out.

She said to me, "You need this."

I wanted to run and hide- well, die was more like it! I was chosen to go to the front of the room.

"Come up here," Dr. Yuen instructed.

Completely mortified, off I went to the front of the room to stand in front of him.

"What is wrong with you?" he asked.

"I have Lyme disease" I replied.

"No, you don't," he stated.

"Yes, I do." I replied.

He said I didn't, but he didn't deal with diagnoses anyway.

"Give me a symptom. Just one," he stated.

I explained I had a strange feeling in my eyes. My vision was fine, but they always felt heavy and very hot inside.

He said, "OK, you have parasites."

I thought, *What the heck is this guy even talking about?* Feeling like he was a nut, I just wanted to get out of there!

"Parasites?" I asked.

He began to move his fingers and hands behind my back without touching me. And suddenly, the hot and weird sensation completely disappeared from my left eye. I thought maybe he was not a crazy person after all. I couldn't believe it. He did the same technique to my right eye. It felt a little different, but not quite the same as the left eye. After having this wild ride of a health challenge, I was very in tune with my body. I knew at that moment my journey to achieve wellness was about to change-for the better. I thanked him and went back to my seat. That night, my eye wasn't going to be the only thing that had a shift. The rest of my journey on this planet was being defined by that experience.

I spoke with Dr. Yuen after the lecture and demonstration for a few minutes. He mentioned to me that he would be in New York City for two weeks and asked if I'd like to come for an appointment. I scheduled an appointment for the following week. When I arrived, I was prepared with a list of a thousand things wrong with my body from the health challenge. I also came prepared with my health history which included as a child; chronic strep throats, which led to lots of antibiotics and a tonsillectomy. That led to other problems, including a compromised immune system. I felt he needed to know the entire picture.

So there I was, in New York City, at my appointment with Dr. Yuen, thinking he was not so crazy now. I put my full confidence in him based on what I'd experienced the night of the lecture and demonstration. My appointment lasted about one and a half hours. He was diligent with my list and went through everything I asked about. When the session was over, I felt wonderful. The lingering symptoms I had were gone. It was amazing. I felt a renewed strength physically, emotionally and spiritually. I had hope.

He mentioned he would be teaching Chinese Energetic Healing, Level I, the following weekend in New York City and recommended I consider taking the class so I "could maintain myself," as he put it.

Being out of work several years, financially devastated and anxious to go to work, I registered immediately. He did say my symptoms may come back a little, but I would learn enough using his method to keep them under control. I was sold and thought, *where had Dr. Yuen been hiding the past several years of my life?*

When I arrived for the Level I class, Dr. Yuen saw me and said I needed a publicist. I had no idea what he was talking about, so I let the thought go out of my mind. My focus was to take his class and keep myself together, so I could get back to work. It was a matter of health and financial wellness, but I never forgot what he said to me. I returned home from the class and decided to try the technique on anyone who would let me. It was intriguing and fun! Dr. Yuen briefly mentioned that this healing method could be used with animals, and there would be a separate class on that. In my infinite wisdom, I decided to try it on my son's rabbit, Snickers. Even though I hadn't taken the animal class yet, I felt the "corrections" could be applied to Snickers.

I thought it would be cool to try this technique on an animal since I thought animals could not possibly know what kind of "corrections" I was making. I reasoned, on some level, that if a human knew healing *could* occur, his or her own mind could foster the results. Snickers be-came my guinea pig, so to speak. She had severe diarrhea problems. The veterinarian hydrated her, gave her antibiotics, and recommended dietary changes. After putting into place what I learned from Dr. Yuen, the "corrections" all pointed to stress. I made the necessary corrections based on what I was finding, and the diarrhea stopped and never came back. In addition, Snickers was not a friendly rabbit. I probably had the only rabbit on the planet that growled, but even that subsided. In retrospect, I could see why the poor little thing was stressed. She was living in the house with four humans (three different generations) and a dog.

So much for ever thinking Dr. Yuen was crazy. He is one of the most intelligent and intuitive people I've ever gotten to know that I truly hold in the highest regard. I learned all levels of his classes and in the late 1990s became certified to teach his system to others. Dr. Yuen thought so highly of me that he offered an opportunity to go to the Shanghai Hospital in China for a couple of weeks with him to work on patients using his system. Unfortunately, I was not able to go.

When I was ready to return to work, the division of the company I worked for in New York had been bought and sold several times and there weren't any positions for me. I decided to work with the Chinese Energetic Healing out of my house for people I knew. Soon people were referring others to me. Eventually, some of my clients began to mention the rays of light coming out from my fingertips. Heat emanated from my palms. I contacted my massage therapist, who also was a Reiki Master and asked her about this. She assured me it was Reiki and attuned me to Reiki Levels I and II. I later was attuned to a Reiki Level III, Master and Teacher. The rays coming out of my fingers were different from Reiki and had nothing to do with Yuen Energetics. It is purely electrical in vibration and it has help people with all kinds of health challenges. Since there was no handbook on this, I prayed to God for guidance on how to help people and animals with this ability.

It was then that I began to hear my *healing* team of angels. They are not my guardian angels. This team is here specifically to help balance energy, which leads to healing. They work through my hands.

As I gave people energy, my awareness of loved ones in Heaven opened even more than it was. Playing soft music, having a few lit candles, and being focused with the angels helped. The afterlife people were flooding into my healing session. I found myself asking my clients if their mom in Heaven had dark curly hair, for example. Nobody but the loved ones in Heaven were ready for communication. I was thankful the client was already lying down as they weren't expecting those visits.

My energy sessions which should have taken an hour or so, were now taking two or three hours. It was too long and exhausting. With help from my angels, I was able to vibrationally separate healing and reading appointments. This meant I could focus on healing for an hour with a client and not entertain people from the other side bombarding me with messages for my client.

It was at this time, that my medical intuition became strong. I saw illnesses, imbalances, and disease inside people's bodies.

In addition to offering energy healing work, I began offering private readings in 2000. In 2001, I also offered group gallery-style readings, that were called "Messages".

Like many people, I've had many challenges. But between my faith in God and my own natural stubbornness, I managed to regain my health, raise my awesome son, start my own business, and because of all of it, I feel I am an inspiration to many people. I drew on my twenty-two years of corporate background and common sense to put together my own business. Please remember, anything is possible!

I've written this guide for you while sitting in Kathleen's log cabin in Bethany, Connecticut, Sonia's house in Jamaica, Vermont, Sandy's beach house in Branford, Connecticut, visiting my son in Santa Barbara, California and at a friend's home in Montreal, Canada. I love doing what I do. I love helping people in my own way. My goal is to offer hope to those who are in need with a healing session, a reading, a lecture, a class, and this book, by working through my heart with love, light and my highest intent.

I have become a more spiritual person as these experiences have brought me to a place closer to God. Without that higher presence, I know I would not be where I am right now. Prayer, faith, and trust have brought me this sense of inner peace and understanding of the laws of the universe, which we are all tapped into.

I am dedicated to helping others spiritually, because of my experiences and inter dimensional insight.

For the sake of this book, here are a few terms to know:

Here refers to people and animals on this planet, "alive", on this plane, and physically able to be seen and heard.

There refers to people, animals, angels, after life people and other beings on - "the other side." - meaning Heaven in the ethers, above us, the Angelic Realm, the Fairy Realm, and other dimensions. These are people and animals that have "transitioned" to Heaven. There means not on the Earth plane.

Transition(ed): is used to refer to a human or animal that has died. I prefer not to use the word "died" or "death" because in my heart of hearts, I don't feel we ever truly die, but we change form. Our soul is an energy that cannot die. As in the laws of physics, energy and matter only change form, and never go away. Therefore, I prefer to use the word "transition."

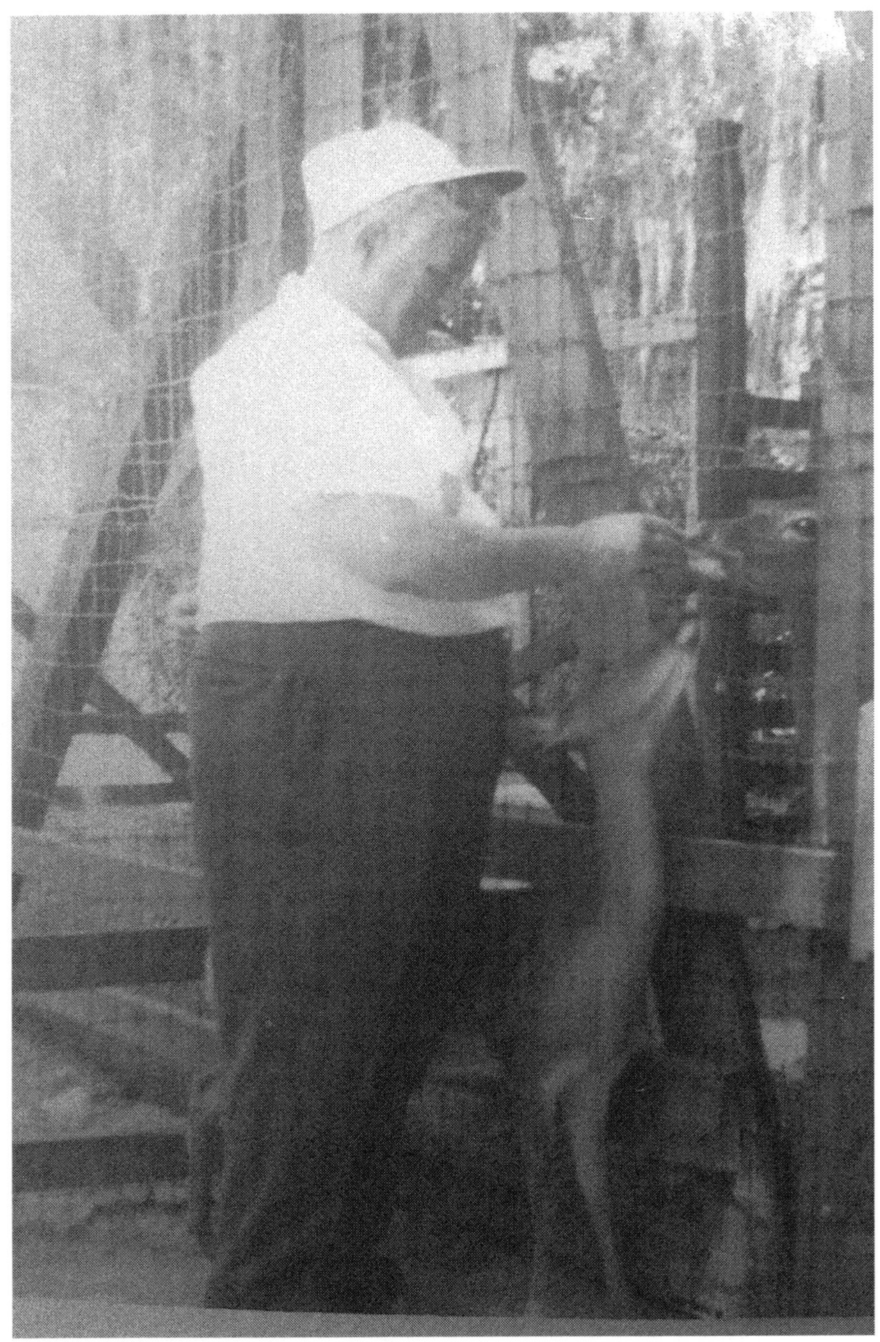

My Grandfather - My Mentor

In January 1964, my beloved Grandfather, Nicholas Louis Squeglia, Sr. left the planet and went to Heaven. It was at that time that I realized I had the ability to see, hear and feel connections with people on the other side that my family could not. I was five years old. They had no idea what I was trying to share with them especially about my grandfather. It was easier to keep this to myself as I became frustrated from the lack of understanding of those around me.

I loved my Papa (my paternal grandfather) with all my heart. When I was a little girl, every Sunday my parents would take me to see my grandparents. He was always happy to see me, and I loved when he held me. On those Sunday mornings, Papa and I would walk several blocks to the local five and dime store in the neighborhood. He always bought me a little doll or toy for ten cents (yes, ten cents). We would sit at the soda fountain counter. He had a cup of coffee and I had my drink of choice, chocolate milk. I loved those Sunday walks with him. It seemed like we spent hours together. When my parents decided to go out for an evening, I was lucky enough to sleep at my grandparent's house. Grandma always had a special blanket for me to sleep on the couch with. We called it the "Indian blanket." It was brightly colored and had an American Indian design. I am blessed to have so many fond memories with them. My sleepovers and Sunday visits with both of my grandparents as well as walks to the store, Papa's smiling face and hugs all abruptly changed when I was five.

When he transitioned to Heaven, it was due to a sudden, massive heart attack in his home. My grandmother witnessed it alone. It happened in the living room. He was standing up from his favorite chair to reach for a cigar and fell to the floor and died instantly. He didn't have a chance of surviving. The call came to our house, and I remember my parent's sheer panic. Nobody had a chance to say good-bye. I never saw Papa physically again.

At the time of my grandfather's transition, my parent's and I lived in Branford, Connecticut. In the days that followed, a lot of people came to visit our house. Everyone was very upset. Some of them were crying. Although there were many people coming in and out, it was very quiet in the house. The grownups talked, planned and there was a certain sense of calm and confusion all at the same time. I noticed people talking about Papa and crying.

I remember this next experience as though it were yesterday. Papa was not buried yet. As I stood in the midst of the confusion, he appeared standing next to me. He stood to my right, looking happy and peaceful as he watched everyone and everything that was going on. He didn't say anything to me. I'll never forget what happened next. As he stood there, he looked at me, smiled, and then looked around at everyone who had come to visit.

I thought to myself, "*Why is everyone so upset? He is right here and looks OK.*"

Calling to my mother I said, "Papa is here!" She said he wasn't. I said he was. She said he wasn't again.

After going back and forth several more times, Mom knelt in front of me and said, "Vanessa, Papa isn't here. He died and went to Heaven."

I tried explaining to her that I already knew that. In fact, I said to her, "I know. He went there first. He is standing right here next to me."

She probably thought I was delusional or making it up. I knew he had gone to Heaven. It felt like he had checked in or registered just as you do if you take a number at a deli.

My grandfather has been with me ever since he transitioned. Even though I was a little girl, I truly believe he and I are soulmates. Papa is always with me and continues to provide me with an enormous amount of comfort and guidance in every aspect of my life. I miss him on this plane, but I know he is there for me. I've learned to ask him for advice and guidance. I love him very much.

More Common Than You Might Think

Many people have experiences with beings from other dimensions which include people and animals from the other side, angels, spirit guides, fairies, power animals, saints, and other icons. All the icons are messengers of God. Just to give you an idea of what these icons are about, here is a general overview. Angels and spirit guides watch over and guide human beings. Fairies look over and govern nature. This includes plants, animals and all that lives in the water. Saints of course are there for human beings and work with God. Power animals guide and assist human beings and are affiliated with the Native American belief system. They are all good, please don't be wary of them.

The thing that strikes me even today is that my grandfather gave me a glimpse of how it was for him at the time of the transition. Through him, I sensed at my young age that he had risen to "Heaven." Not only did he transition quickly, but he was able to visit me anytime he chose. This is the best way I can describe it. He could see and hear everything that was going on and was just as loving as always. He looked as he did when I saw him last wearing the same clothes. Another experience that comes to my mind, was in the sixth grade, my friends and I decided to have a séance. My friend Paula was upset because her godmother had committed suicide. In my infinite wisdom, I suggested we contact her. The godmother came through and super imposed her face on one of my other girlfriends. Nobody saw it but me. It was hard to describe to my friends. When I tried to describe to them what was happening, my friend Laura because so frightened, she ran up the stairs to get away. *How does one explain this to a person who can't see the same things?* I thought.

As I mentioned earlier, I realized early on that other people didn't have the same experiences as I had with the afterlife people. It was never a scary thing to me. Because I didn't share this gift with others until later in my life, I felt very isolated a lot of the time. I wasn't an introvert, as I had many friends and was involved with a lot of activities. I just didn't talk about my spiritual side or what I was seeing. There was nobody to share it with. I got used to feeling that way. Being psychically gifted in any way, can be a lonely place sometimes. If you have ever felt that way, you know exactly what I mean. The great news is that the awareness of God given spiritual gifts are increasing by the second for many of us. I recommend if you are feeling this way, you are not alone. Find likeminded people to share your experiences and spiritual growth with.

Based on my own experience with afterlife people, as my angels refer to them, there is somewhere else we travel to after we leave this existence. It comforts me to know we go to Heaven after this existance.

In the mid 1990's, my angels encouraged me to go public with these gifts. I resisted at first because I was unsure I would be able to do a good job of conveying important messages from their loved ones in Heaven. But as time went on, I conceded to come out of the psychic closet. It is such a normal way of life for me now. I love being able to help people in this way.

Part II – Angels and Other Miscellaneous Tidbits

God and the Angels

Angels are God's messengers from Heaven. They oversee all human beings. There are many levels or bands of angels and they all report directly to God. These beings are depicted in almost every religion. Most often, they are thought to have wings, but sometimes we have Earth angels. Earth angels can take human form and they also can be real people. They come in and out of our lives to assist us with our lessons all the time. Most folks have had experiences of a person coming into their life for either a long or short period of time. Then suddenly, they aren't there for one reason or another. People come in and out of our lives to help us with our spiritual lessons and when those lessons are complete, they leave. Again, these people can be your Earth angels.

Angels constantly give us signs that they are all around us. You may hear a song about angels. You may smell a sweet rosy fragrance. Anytime you notice three of the same numbers in a row, for example 444, you know your guardian angels are close by. Your guardian angels are assigned to only you by God. They are not shared with anyone else. They always want you to know they are with you, helping and loving you. Try to think of them as a best friend you may never see. They unconditionally love you no matter what. Ask them for help at any time.

Guidance from My Own Teams of Angels

At the time of my health challenge in the 1990's, I not only learned to get my body stronger, but I came to realize that there were angels and not just loved ones around us (such as my grandfather). Because I was mis-diagnosed several times by several doctors, I eventually sought spiritual counseling to see if I could give get any insight that the medical doctors may have been missing. I met with a psychic, and specifically asked her to meditate to know if I should be taking any herbs. I felt that I should, but I wasn't hearing the names of the herbs myself. After a little while, my angels suggested Gotu Kola to the psychic. Neither she nor I had heard of it. I went forth with the information, and presented it to a homeopathic doctor in New Haven, Connecticut. She informed me that it was useful for the nervous sys-tem. One of the effects of what I was experiencing had an impact on my nervous system. I found the herb and began to take it. It proved to be helpful, and I was grateful for the information that put me one step closer to feeling myself again.

Where did that information come from? My own team of angels. Nobody knows us like our angels. After that incident, I heard about a psychic in Branford, Connecticut who did readings. I feel ashamed that I cannot remember her name. I made an appointment with her, and when I arrived I sat in her living room. The first thing she addressed was my health since it was my biggest concern. She began by telling me my "health" angel's name-Titus.

I said, "What are you talking about?"

She was surprised that I had no awareness of him. I had never heard his name. I knew I had angels though. She said he had been around me since I'd gotten sick. He was huge and strong. She said at that moment, he was leaning on my left shoulder. I quickly brought my attention and awareness to my left shoulder and I felt pressure there. She went on to say that he was also sometimes learning right along with me about the non-conventional therapies I was exploring to get better. Apparently, he liked the idea of my trying Tai Chi. She told me he had helped me with a Tai Chi move, and I remembered what she was referring to. There is no way she would have known this. When I was practicing in my Tai Chi class, I was doing everything backwards. I was laughing at myself. All of a sudden, one of my feet turned into a certain position, and I felt a thrust of energy run through my body.

Oh, I finally got it, I had thought to myself.

I was so proud that I did it correctly. As it turned out, it wasn't me at all. It was Titus. He took full credit for helping me with the positioning of my feet.

The Branford psychic mentioned another time that Titus helped me. It was when I was receiving acupuncture. The doctor had asked me if I wanted a Shiatsu massage on my back. Not knowing the difference in massage therapies, I quickly said yes. I thought it was like Swedish massage and I would feel relaxed. I learned very quickly that it was something very different. There were times throughout that health challenge that my skin hurt to the touch. Sometimes it hurt to take a shower. As I was still lying on the massage table after my acupuncture session, the doctor began to pound my back. Suddenly, my left arm seemed to have a mind of its own. It reached up and stopped the doctor from taking one more chop at my back. He stopped, and I felt very relieved to say the least. The psychic began to recite that exact story. Titus was the one who lifted my arm to stop the doctor from pounding again. The psychic changed my way of thinking spiritually. If she ever reads this, I hope she feels the impact she had on my life relating to angels and knows how thankful I am to her. She helped open spiritual doors that I needed at that time. I'm also eternally grateful to Titus, who is still with me today, despite his challenges of watching over the stubborn human being he was assigned. As I became more tuned in with the angels, I realized I had so many of them. They appeared and talked to me in groups. Some of them were to help me with health and healing and some were there to help with other areas of my life. I then realized I had my very own teams of angels. I began to thank them daily for continuing to support me and offer guidance whenever I need them.

I've made up a little diagram of how angels, humans, afterlife people as well as other dimensions are all connected to God. God is the hub of the cosmic universe. It is the all-knowing energy that binds all of us together. It is from God's energy that we all receive our own infinite wisdom and where as we evolve ethically, morally, and spiritually. We will climb to our highest potential to be one with God. An infinite power of love and wisdom connect all these realms. Quiet time, meditation, prayer, and breath-work all help us to stay aligned and connected with God. Any way you can stay aligned is helpful for your overall well-being. It can even help you develop your own intuition. I like to think of a bicycle wheel for an example. God is the hub, or center of the wheel. Then all the other dimensions connected to the hub are the spokes, which always connect and draw on the hub's energy for support, wisdom, and energy.

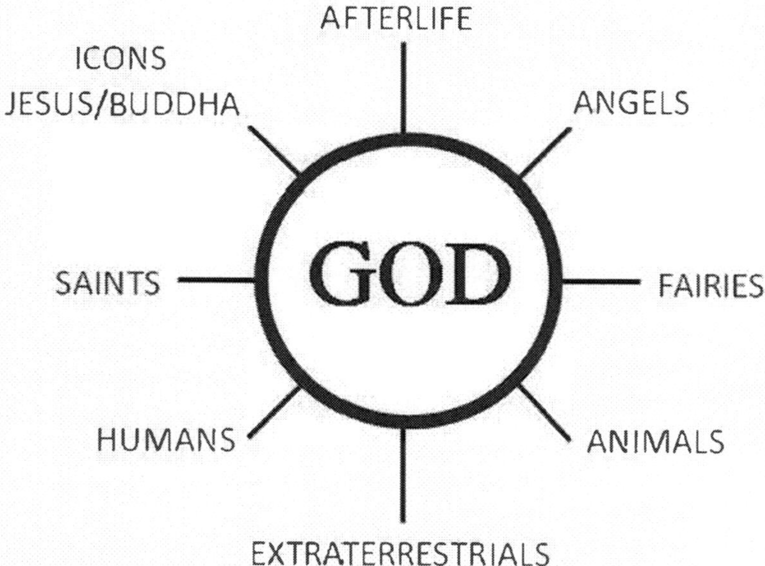
AFTERLIFE
ICONS
JESUS/BUDDHA
ANGELS
GOD
SAINTS
FAIRIES
HUMANS
ANIMALS
EXTRATERRESTRIALS

What Is the Difference Between an Angel and One of Our Loved Ones in Heaven?

It has been shown to me that angels and loved ones or afterlife people, "live" in two different realms. Each type of heavenly being has a designated dimension, but all report to God. We live on Earth but are connected to God. Angels and those in the afterlife have similar responsibilities, such as watching over and helping people they are connected to. They love to help us in any way they can. It's always important to ask them for help. One of the Laws of the Universe is that they are unable to help us unless we ask them. The only exception to that is if it is a life threatening circumstance and it's truly not our time to go to Heaven. The help us by giving us signs through our thoughts and many other ways. You will begin to understand the various dimensions we have available to help us.

I'd like you to see a very easy way to conceptualize the "food chain" of the universe with God being at the top. The lower levels of Heaven are where people go if they haven't been good, moral, and ethical people. People who have committed suicide fall into this category as well, not because they are bad people. You can read more about that in the Suicide Chapter. Most people will be in levels four through seven. The saints, Mother Theresa and other people who have dedicated their lives serving God to help humanity, will be in level eight, as well as all the various angels, including the archangels. They all report directly to

God and watch over us. The top level is God, which I categorize as level 10. I find that people can move in and out of the different levels according to their soul's journey. This happens in many ways and is explained in other chapters.

Heavenly Ladder

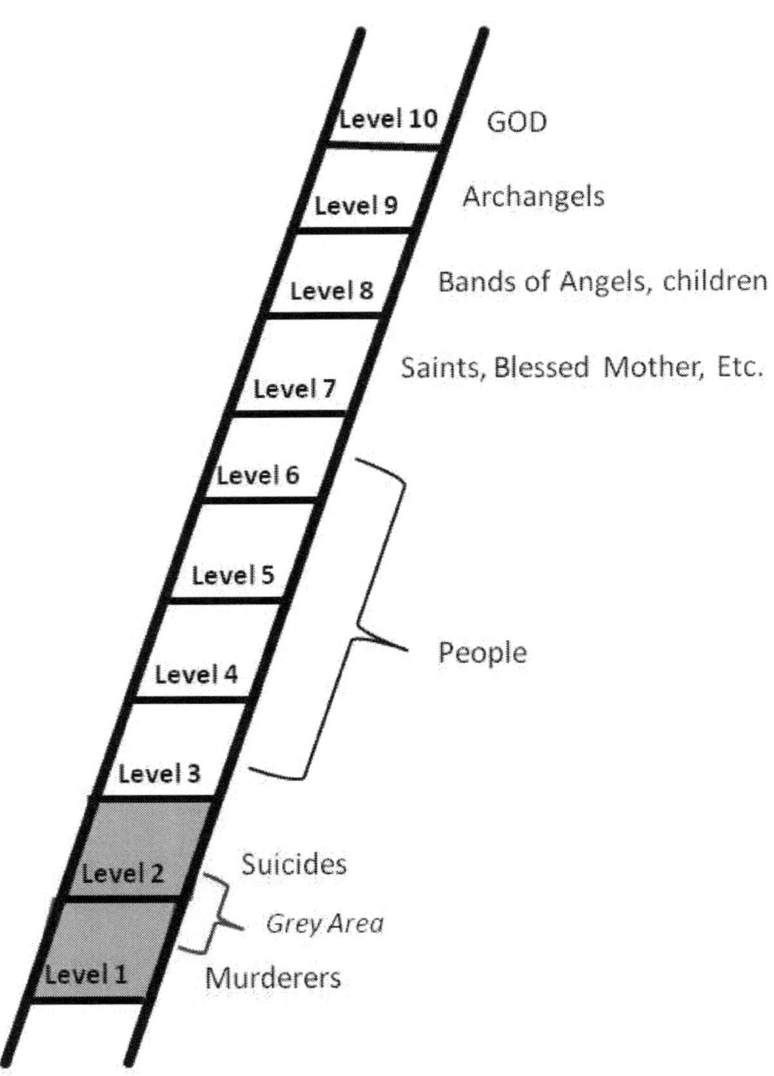

Free Will

I've learned so much along my life's journey. There have been times when I have made better decisions than others, as most of us have. Sometimes my angels recommended the decisions I was making weren't the best and not for my highest good. But, I still went ahead with what I wanted to do and found myself regretting not listening to my angel's advice. Then other times have been right on point.

Let's talk about free will. It is a ***gift*** from God. This is one of the biggest blessings of being a human being. We can decide many things for ourselves. Before you were born, you made a choice with God and decided where in this world you were going to live and different experiences you would have. The decisions continue daily. Decisions can be as simple as what to eat or what to wear, to what type of job to have, and even what type of place to live. We choose our friends, our life partners, and our pets. People can suggest what they think you should be doing with your life, but only you can make your own decisions. God, the angels, your loved ones on the other side and other guides are not allowed to make decisions for us. They can however, help guide you to make the best decisions. You may not hear words as I do, but you may have a gut feeling, a dream, an idea that seems to come out of nowhere. Please pay attention. Your angels and afterlife people may be trying to guide you to take the best route on your journey here on Earth.

Wouldn't life seem easier if someone would say, do this or that with your life, especially in times of big decision making? Decisions we make throughout our lives help us move forward on our spiritual paths. Some common lessons are learning to trust, have faith, have high self-esteem, patience and many more. In my spiritual counseling, I can help you to make your own decision by providing insight into what will happen if you go one route verses another route on your life path. I always let my clients know the decisions are up to them.

Chakra System

There are hundreds of books written on the Chakra system. For those who do not know what a chakra is, allow me to explain. A chakra is an energy center that is connected to your etheric body or aura which is the energy field outside of your physical body. Each chakra corresponds to different organs and parts of your body. There are seven major chakras that line up though out the torso and head. They each have specific colors and spin in a certain direction. The brighter and faster the chakras are, the healthier we feel. If a chakra is not "spinning" properly or isn't as bright as it should be, it can cause an imbalance in the physical body which can result in imbalance making us not feel well. It doesn't take much to disrupt the chakra system. Emotional upsets, eating improperly, and stress are just a few factors that can keep a chakra in an imperfect state. Meditation, good eating habits, plenty of hydration, body and energy work, exercise, proper rest, and a positive outlook all help to keep our chakras balanced. There is a lot of information available on the chakra system in books and on the internet if you wish to educate yourself about the chakra system. It is fascinating.

The specific chakra I want to talk about is the heart chakra as it pertains to our emotional self, which is our happiness and sadness and every emotion in between. This one is very important for you to understand. It is positioned in the middle of the chest and is referred to as our emotional heart center. The heart chakra radiates pink and green energies or colors. Again, it corresponds to all emotions. When we experience life's challenges, whether it be grief, moving, changing jobs, worrying, or any other shifts, our heart chakra is affected. As everyone knows, we can only handle so much stress. Under stress, the heart chakra changes by spinning slowly and its brightness dims. This creates an unbalanced energetic disruption. Almost anything can alter the heart chakra. Just turn on the news these days. This spiritual emotional center in our body can experience an energetic block. This happens to protect us from any more trauma and even grief. You may not even notice it. When the heart chakra is not balanced, it is a little more difficult for afterlife people to connect with us. After someone we love goes to Heaven, we can still have some unresolved questions about the decisions we had to make which may create guilt, self-doubt, and many other emotions. We generally miss them, creating sadness. It all affects the heart chakra in some way. This is all normal. It is perfectly fine to go through a grieving process which is different for everyone. If you find yourself not able to return to day-to-day living after a while, please reach out to a grief counselor or therapist. You may consider a support group that is appropriate to your specific type of loss. For example, losing a child, a spouse, a parent or even a pet.

Reincarnation

Been there done that!

The subject of reincarnation fascinates me. Because there is so much written on reincarnation and I am asked about it often, I wanted to gently mention it. Reincarnation means that you have lived before in another time and place. You can be a male or female. Each lifetime you may be a different ethnicity. The point of reincarnation is to experience anything that you can to enhance your soul on its spiritual journey. We generally come back with the same groups of people, such as family for instance. Coworkers, friends, and animals are other examples. We can change our roles depending on what lessons are needed while we are still in Heaven.

I'm sure you have had an experience like the following: When you meet someone new, you know instantly if you really like them or not. Your immediate thought is "Hey, this person is awesome". Something clicks. Or, it may be just the opposite experience. You may feel you have an aversion to a person. If you experience any kind of aversion, please follow your instinct. This person may not be for your highest good. Either way, there is a karmic connection. When a positive connection is made, there is a definite desire to get to know that person. It doesn't have to be a romantic partner. Relationships include family, friends, lovers, co-workers and even animals.

These connections happen to all of us very often. Here is a common example that I find. You meet someone and fall for them romantically. There is one problem. The problem is one or both of you are in a committed relationship (i.e.: marriage). There is an uncontrollable urge to be together. You both know it makes no sense and neither of you has been outside your marriage before this. It continues for any length of time. There is a certain spark. You both know it is wrong. Then all the feelings of guilt and everything else that couples with an emotional and/or physical affair, come to the surface. When this kind of relationship ignites, there is a very good reason it happens. I'm simply trying to put this into a karmic explanation. When this happens, both of you had a prior existence together, a past life. Since we come together in groups, it's most likely this person could have been a spouse, partner even a lover in another existance. Although we are in a different incarnation in a different body, our soul remains the same. It carries a spiritual path and karmic lessons. Our soul is who we are. It evolves with learning life lessons. In this instance, two people are here together again, but not necessarily to re-experience themselves on a physical level. There are here to support one another perhaps with some of each other's life lessons.

I have an example of this in my own life. Years ago, I met a fella name Joe (the first name is changed). We met at a spiritual group we both used to attend, and we clicked right away. Luckily, both he and I are very intuitive and are also healers. Our friendship began to grow. To say there wasn't a spark would be a lie. Anyone who saw us together thought we were married. We were, but not in this lifetime! He and I would give each other healing work from time to time. What unfolded in some of those sessions was amazing. Sometimes we would see our past lives simultaneously. At one point early in our friendship, we made a conscious decision that this is not the lifetime to be romantically involved. I've learned over the years that I've known this man before, that he is always there for me and I will always be there for him. We have had many shared existences together. But this one is supposed to be supportive of our experiences and journeys on this Earth plane this time around. Even when we don't talk or see each other for long periods of time, we always pick up where we left off. As though there was never a gap in time. With that type of karmic connection, picking back up is easy.

Part III – About Heaven

Afterlife 101

About Afterlife People

First, after life people are thrilled to be able to connect with people *here*. Even though this was written earlier in the book, I wanted to reiterate it.

Here refers to people and animals on this plane, "alive", on this plane, and physically able to be seen and heard.

There refers to people, animals, angels, after life people and other beings on - "the other side." – in Heaven. They are not on the Earth plane.

Transition(ed) refers to a human or animal that has died. I prefer not to use the word "died" or "death" because in my heart of hearts, I don't feel we ever truly die, but we change form. Our soul is an energy that cannot die. As in the laws of physics, energy and matter only change form, and never go away. I prefer to use the word "transition."

The majority of transitioned people are fine. The percentage of people not fine is very small. In all the time I have read professionally, I have only seen a handful of people who did not transition. Luckily, I was able to help and guide them into Heaven.

There are commonalities in many of my readings as far as who meets us when we transition. I always see what I refer to as, the "front line". It is made up of the people who were the closest to us on Earth and who are already in Heaven. They can be our spouses, parents, grandparents, siblings, children, friends, co-workers, neighbors and even our animals. We recognize them right away. They encourage the transition process by letting us know they are happy to see us, and by welcoming us into Heaven. I'll see pets directly in front of the people standing in the center of the front line. Off to the side of the family members, I see friends, neighbors, and co-workers. Behind the front line, I'll see grandparents and their generational line, great grandparents behind them and so forth. There will be family members you may not have known while you were *here,* but, they know you. They watch over families for generations. You will recognize the people that you didn't get to know *here* when you arrive in Heaven. This also occurs when you meet your angels and any icons such as Jesus, Buddha and of course God.

During one reading, a little boy came to me. He was about eight or nine-years-old, and he was sopping wet and bluish in color. I knew right away that he was lost. My client verified that she knew nothing of the child. He had drowned, and for many years he was in a limbo state. He had seen my light and told me he had been looking for his mother. I guided him through the light to his grandmother. It took me a few minutes to convince the little boy to go with his grandmother. After explaining it was the only way to find his own mother, he moved into the light where his grandmother lovingly took him. I was able to check in on him later that evening and he was happy and well. He was not discolored and wet. Are there souls that are lost? Yes. But, as previously mentioned, the majority of people that talk to me are perfectly fine in Heaven!

Common Questions about the Afterlife

There are so many questions I've heard over the years. I have provided the answers to a few of the most common ones that I felt might be of interest.

Are We Ever Really Alone?

Hardly! Sometimes people need to transition to Heaven very unexpectedly. We may not be able to be with them. There could have been a tragic accident. Very often, when a person is on the cusp of transitioning and has visitors that leave the room for even a few moments, he or she will transition to Heaven. This happens because he or she may not want the family members or friends to witness their last breath. That is how they feel. If a person transitions unexpectedly from an accident, a murder, a drug overdose, a medical mishap or even a heart attack they are not alone. Most people think these folks are all alone when things like that happen. While they may be alone on this plane, there are always afterlife people, angels, and other beings around them that know what is happening and are ready to meet them.

The angels have encouraged me to refer to this as "the pickup." Whatever your religious belief system is, you will be met by what you believe in and prayed to, if you prayed. I see pickups all the time, it is beautiful.

Only one time in my history of reading, did I have an atheist come to see me for a reading. I didn't understand why someone with the belief that there is no Heaven would be interested in what I do and want to connect to a loved one who transitioned, but I went forward with the reading. During the session, her afterlife people visited. After a lot of tears by my client, I knew everything made sense to her. I am positive she left the reading with a new outlook.

Our loved ones in Heaven are delighted to let us know who they are with. Many people in Heaven have told me that they thought about Heaven when they were alive. They knew it existed but didn't understand that our souls never die. The possibility of meeting up with the love of their life, family members, friends and pets in Heaven never entered their thoughts. When they arrived in Heaven, they were surprised shocked and very happy to see everyone *there.* I get goose bumps every time I hear that.

Do We Have to See People We Didn't Like?

Most likely, but even if we didn't have the best relationships with some of our relatives, friends, they will want to greet us in a loving manner. Most times, we are happy to see each other despite any differences that may have taken place. This doesn't mean you have to hang around them for all of eternity. If there were major differences in opinions, fighting, or even abuse, there is plenty of time in Heaven to work on those conflicts. You may decide to come back later in another life to work out the differences. Reincarnation is an option if you all choose to do that.

What Happens if I Am Divorced? Do I Have to be with My Ex-Spouse?

No. As stated before, you may not want to address the issue(s) that made life with that person such a struggle when you were together as soon as you get to Heaven. Perhaps you may not want to work out the issues at all. Either way is OK. However, you will have to work out your differences to satisfy karma at some point. You can do that during the next lifetime or wait several lifetimes. Don't let that worry you now, though. I have seen spouses on the other side coming to visit their children together just for the sake of the reading, despite their own issues between themselves. Other times, I have seen spouses that have come together in a reading who have worked out their issues on the other side. They may not be in love, but they are amicable and respectful of each other.

My first spouse (partner) transitioned, and I remarried or found another life partner. What will happen in Heaven? Will I be able to be with my first love?

You will see your first spouse or partner. They will be there waiting for you for at the *pickup* along with your other family members and angels to guide you to Heaven. You will have the best of both worlds when all of you are *there.* Your sweethearts will take care of you and love you. I have seen this over and over again. Jealousy, anger, and most of the human emotions that consume and debilitate us while we are still here disappear. I hear often from a spouse or partner in Heaven encouraging the one still *here* to go on a date or at least out for coffee. It makes the afterlife happy to see us staying connected to other human beings after they transition.

Here is a true story about meeting new people after a spouse transitions: Someone I know lost her husband without warning. It was devastating for her. She decided to join a grief support group at a local hospice to help her through the stages of grieving and be with some people experiencing the same. It was here that she met new friends that she could relate to. She met a woman who became a new found, exquisite friend.

That new friend who was in her mid-eighties at the time, had also lost her husband. She was a devout Catholic was a devoted wife of many years. Her devotion led her to feel comforted while visiting her husband's grave daily. Every time she was at the cemetery, she would see a man visiting a grave site nearby. She and the man finally spoke to each other. It was then that she learned he had lost his devoted wife. For six months, he asked her every day to go for coffee. She always politely declined. But he was persistent and she accepted the offer. The pair hit it off and were inseparable. I had the opportunity to meet them both. One night, my friend, this couple and I attended a local fundraising dance. It was almost midnight, and those two were still dancing the night away like two twenty-five-year old's. I was ready to leave by half past eleven. They both amazed me and were such an inspiration because they were enjoying life to its fullest. I truly feel that both of their beloved spouses had everything to do with bringing them together. Don't ever think you are too old to love again. This couple was living proof of that.

What if I Don't Want to Hear from Someone on the Other Side and He or She Comes to Visit Me?

This situation does come up occasionally. Sometimes when an afterlife person comes to me to talk to my client during a reading, the client reacts in an angry way and lets me know why and how much they hated the person on the other side. Or they don't want to connect due to unresolved issues. My client usually has a justifiable reason for feeling this way. It could have been anything. So, I have a person in Heaven who wants to say something to my client, and the client isn't interested in the connection. It's quite awkward for me because I am in the middle. I then must either ask the afterlife person to leave my line of view. More often than not, these souls want to express their sorrow, remorse, or just say that they are sorry for something. I have seen afterlife people down on one knee asking for forgiveness. Many times, my clients who haven't had healthy relationships with some of their loved ones, will let those on the other side voice themselves. In doing spiritual work with so many people, some folks just get caught up in bad habits or neglectful situations for one reason or another. When one of them is on the other side and issues haven't been resolved, an emotional wake is left behind, which results in an emotional roller coaster. But those who have transitioned, have a sense of clarity. Teams of mentoring angels help with "could haves," "should haves," and "would haves." Afterlife people are aware that different choices could have led to different outcomes in their lives. The afterlife people tell me that they had forgotten a lot of the little things until they are shown by their teams of angels. I recently had a situation like this.

A client from New York City came in for a reading many years ago. Her biological father and her step father popped in. When she realized her natural father was waiting to speak to her, she adamantly refused the connection. He had been an alcoholic, and there were many unresolved issues between them. He presented to me in a loving way, but I also had to honor my client's wish. I reluctantly sent him away from my line of sight. If only she had welcomed him in for even a moment, I felt he was going to try to clear the air. Those who have transitioned can do emotional damage control for those still *here*. We continued with the reading and she was very pleased to hear from her stepfather who thought of her as his own daughter.

What Are Afterlife People Doing?

Our loved ones over *there* have responsibilities.

God assigns jobs when we are ready, which can include helping people both in Heaven and on Earth. They are not only looking over us, and they certainly don't rest. The don't rest because they don't need to. They are already plugged in and since they don't have a physical body anymore, they don't get tired. In addition to watching over us, they work on their own spiritual journey, have jobs assigned by God and more. This is so out of the box and abstract. Like God, they can be in more than one place at a time. That means they can visit us, work on their own soul's journey and help God with what is needed.

They are always guiding and helping us. However, they cannot make decisions for us because we have free will, as I mentioned earlier in the book. Free will gives us the ability to make our own choices. Afterlife people can help us all the time, but they are not allowed to help until we ask for help. The only exception is that there is a life-threatening circumstance and it is not our time to go to Heaven, just the same as the angels.

I've had a few experiences like this myself, one of which I'd like to share with you. In February 2000, I was in a car accident with my son on a Friday night. We were traveling north on I-95 in New Haven, Connecticut, just at the split of I-91 and I-95. There was a problem with the passenger car door. I pulled into the "V" section of the split in the highway to check the door. My son, Shane, was about twelve years old at the time. I was driving my two-year-old car, which was my favorite color – purple. Within seconds after pulling into the "V", I put my flashers on and stopped the car. I happened to look into my rear-view mirror and saw two headlights coming directly towards us. I thought to myself (and this happened so fast it was probably nanoseconds), that if I were to die in a car crash after all I'd been through in the last ten years or so, I was going to be very be mad! I then called to God to help.

I remember saying aloud; and without fear, "GOD, HELP US NOW." Just then, the headlights I saw crashed into the back of my car. The air bags didn't go off. My car was crunched like an accordion.

Here are some of the miracles of that night. I felt my car lift from behind. The car that rear-ended me was sent backwards about twenty feet. My head and body did not hit the steering wheel. Since I am short, that was surprising. Shane and I were barely injured. I ended up with some damage to my forearms, but I'm convinced it was because I braced the steering wheel when I saw what was about to happen from the mirror. I had the two rear seats down and had a bunch of stuff in the trunk. Everything that was in the trunk came up within an inch or two of the back of the front seats. Anyone involved in this accident should have been seriously injured.

More to the story...

Right after the crash, an ambulance which had just finished working for the night was on its way back to the garage, stopped at the scene of the accident without being called. The ambulance driver, after seeing the car looking like an accordion, radioed the fire department, which in turn, had used the "jaws of life" to cut us out of the car. We were then whisked off to Yale New Haven Hospital where my son and I were checked and released. The hospital classified the accident as a minor accident. They obviously didn't see the car.

It was neither Shane's nor my time to leave the planet. God and our teams of angels, archangels, guides and loved ones all surrounded us with a buffering energy.

I have a friend in Arizona who is also a psychic. When I spoke with her after the accident, she told me that some of the archangels were not particularly thrilled with my decision to pull the car over where I did. They knew what was about to happen and were ready to cushion the blow to us and the car. Another odd part after it was over was that the

New Haven Fire Department had no record of using the Jaws of Life on my car, but it happened. As the firefighters were cutting off the door so we could get out of the car, Shane said, "This is really cool." I was crying because I was so upset, I yelled "this is not cool!" One funny part of this story was that my grandmother was watching the local eleven o'clock news. My accident was on TV and she recognized my car. Gram never missed a thing. She was born in 1910 and sharp as a tack until the day she transitioned at age 104. Here is a picture of my Gramma just before she transitioned.

Several weeks after the accident I was still upset that my car had been taken away from me because of the accident and that is when I had a dream of Jesus hanging on a wall crucifix. His eyes watched me carefully. In the dream, everywhere I walked he stared at me from that cross. I found myself yelling at Jesus in the dream and questioning him.

"Why did you take the car?"

"How am I supposed to get around?"

"How was I supposed to bring Shane to school?"

Jesus had his eyes fixated on me, stated with conviction, "I COULD HAVE TAKEN YOU AND YOUR SON. I TOOK THE CAR INSTEAD."

I woke up suddenly, completely startled and in a sweat, realizing I just had a visit from Jesus and he made a valid point. I never complained about the loss of the car again. Things can always be replaced. People cannot. He was probably so sick and tired of hearing me complain. I will never forget his visit. To say I was humbled, would be an understatement.

How do people look over *"there"*?

If you take nothing else away from this book, please remember the way I see Heaven. There is no sickness, no injuries, sadness or arguing. I have never seen a rainy day either, except one time, I was shown snow. Everyone is fine! There are very few exceptions. I can count those folks on one hand. They also appear to me at the age they felt they looked their best. I've seen people of all ages. Your grandmother may show herself to me at age 25. We like to project ourselves younger from over there. Conversely, children have come to me from the afterlife at their current age, not at the age of their transition. I've also seen the afterlife appearing as exquisite balls of light.

Many years ago, I was working at a psychic fair in Newport, Rhode Island. A woman requested a reading. She wanted to hear from her "baby boy".

I heard a deep voice from say, "tell her I'm not a baby anymore, I'm twenty-seven".

I repeated what I'd heard. She confirmed that would be his current age. The "baby boy" told me what he had been doing in Heaven. He went to school and was with many of her relatives. He asked her not to worry so much about him. The mom expressed gratitude for the reading. She also was a bit perplexed. It was difficult for her to picture her "baby boy" as a grown man. She had held him in her heart and thoughts as an infant for 27 years. I reassured her to think of him in the way that gave her the most comfort. It was her son's way of validating who he was at that moment.

Some people can't walk prior to their transition. Their faces glow as they walk for me when they talk to me from Heaven. Others who had experienced lung problems, share with me their new ability to breathe. They let me know of changes to their physical appearance, including body weight. Those who had hair loss, proudly display their enviable full head of hair. People who were exhausted feel a renewed feeling of energy.

Cognitive difficulties no longer exist. Those who suffered with Alzheimer's disease, dementia, been in a coma or were over medicated are amazed at the clarity of their thoughts in Heaven.

Heaven's kitchen is always open for business. It features the freshest produce; the most decadent sauces and sweets are delightful. Diabetics are thrilled with what they can eat now. It's always easy for me to detect a diabetic on the other side, because mounds of goodies surround them. And no meal is complete without a favorite cocktail or fine wine and after dinner cigarette. There are no repercussions for unhealthy habits in Heaven.

It's always comforting for me to see the relief on the faces of those who have entrusted me with the honor of giving them their reading.

Styling 101

Afterlife people dress in clothes typical of their own style. Sometimes they appear very dressed up and in the next blink they are casually dressed.

If you didn't know the afterlife person, but you know of them, they will appear in an outfit you have a picture of them wearing and at the age they were in the picture. The purpose is to help identify who is connecting. You may have been looking at photos with other family members trying to figure out who everyone is. Let's say a woman in a picture you were looking at had a blue dress with a white collar, pearls and had short curly hair. You are having a medium reading. This woman in the photo decides to visit wearing the same outfit as in the picture. Voila! We made a connection that this is your great grandmother. Even though you may have never met her, she wants you to know she is watching over you.

I've seen people wearing beach clothes, walking barefoot, wearing sneakers, high heels, dress shoes and even boat shoes. They love to change their outfits throughout the reading also. It's interesting and always makes sense to my clients. That's all that counts.

How They Give Us Signs of Their Presence

Feeling Their Presence

Guess what? You are not losing your mind!

Simply feeling someone's presence is *the* most common way they connect with us. You may not be able to see where they are. But you *know* they are there. Please learn to trust your feelings and know that you are not making it up. I find that so often people have this experience and they think "Oh, I'm just missing them", or "Oh, I'm making this up, it's my imagination", or "It can't be".

We miss our loved ones so much that we think we are creating these feelings. We don't create it. We sense them. We feel them. I must mention at this point it is *never* a scary feeling. You will feel warm and comforted. You are not imagining it.

You may never see or hear them and that's OK. I know those in the afterlife take such delight in acknowledgement, so please don't forget to thank them for being there.

Thanking them being around can be offered in many ways. If you can say thanks aloud, that is great! Of course, you should not do this if you are in a public. Use your thoughts to say thanks. They will understand because they are connected to us through our heart and our thoughts. There is no right or wrong way to express your gratitude to them. Whatever you feel most comfortable with will work!

Visiting Us in Dreams

We are all very busy in our daily lives, running at a very fast pace and juggling many things at once. We all have many things to accomplish in a short amount of time and people live a life full of many worries. Because of these daily distractions, it is difficult for us to receive signs from our loved ones. Sometimes they decide to visit us during our sleep state in the form of dreams. They are not always dreams, however. Normally they are "visits" from the afterlife. Here is the difference between a dream and a "visit".

Dreams

After waking from a "dream", you may not recall it in its entirety. It is vague. You will recall only bits and pieces of the dream. In addition, if you do remember the dream, it fades over time.

Visits

When you wake after having a visit, you remember everything very clearly. You can recall every detail, including where the visit was, and who they were with. It seems as real as can be, and unlike dreams, you don't forget it. Sometimes these visits are so real that the memory of it can last for years yet seem like it was just last night. The visit can be remembered in its entirety and it may or may not be in familiar setting or somewhere you know. You may see them with people you know or people you don't recognize. They may be by themselves. If you hear them speaking to you, you will remember exactly what they said. A common connection you may hear is that they are OK, they love you or they can offer you advice on a decision or circumstance you have going on. Feel blessed with these experiences. It can be compared to talking on a cell phone. Sometimes when they speak to us it can be very clear and sometimes not. But the memory of how they look and where they are is as clear as can be.

I often have people tell me they saw a loved one during a "dream" which is really a visit. They say that the loved one just stood in place, staring at them. People ask me if something ominous is going to happen. For example, let's say your mom came to you last night and just stood there, not saying a word. First of all, relax. This is not a bad thing. Most people don't realize the afterlife people don't use their mouths to speak like we do. Communication is all done telepathically. Simply put again, it just means their thoughts and hearts are connecting with your thoughts and heart.

If you want to make a clear connection, here is what I recommend. Before going to sleep, ask whomever you want to connect with to speak louder and you will try harder to listen. You can say this outload or in your head. They can show up whenever they want, and visits can be frequent or infrequent. Try not to get frustrated. It can happen very randomly. The fact is that you never really know what their agenda is since it is their show! You will be surprised. It works. When they visit again you will have a clearer connection.

Don't be afraid. These are people who love you and whom you love. They may just say hello, or they may communicate more information. Remember that, it all depends on the communication connections between you and them. Since it may be new to them also, they might think you understand their communication. Once again, by setting your intentions of listening to them on a subconscious level helps them as well.

I want to share a story with you about one of my angelic healing team members – Thomas. Although I am deferring to an angelic experience and was fully awake at the time, the concept is the same. In the summer of 2000, I was facilitating an energy healing session for a woman. Just prior to the session, we had a mini-consultation of what was going on with her, so that I could focus the healing energies on the issues at hand. She had fibromyalgia. The session began as usual. About halfway into the session, I heard a faint whisper directing me to "go to her left shoulder – there is pain there." I thought I was losing my mind! All the other angelic healing team members that worked with me during energy work up to that point are quite loud; Patrick, who thinks he is a comedian. I asked my client if, in fact, her left shoulder was a problem for her. She said "yes" and that she forgot to let me know. I directed "THE" Healing Energy (as my angels want to me convey this vibration of energy transmission) to her left shoulder. After the session was over and my client left, I decided to have a little chat (although it sound-ed like a one-way conversation to me at first) with the angel who had whispered to me. I wasn't sure who it was at that time. But, I asked the voice to talk a little bit louder to me and I would do my best to listen to him. It worked. This was my first awareness of Thomas, a new angelic healing team member. He told me he wasn't sure how loud to talk. He still speaks softer than the rest, but communication is much easier since we had our chat.

You need to tell your loved ones on the other side the same thing. Remind them to speak louder and you will listen better while you sleep. Again, it works. And remember, you may receive a brief message of "I am OK", "I love you" or a much longer message.

Another key point about these visits is that, sometimes, your loved ones will visit someone else that won't get as upset as you might. I'll use the example of mom on the other side again. Mom visits one of your, cousins during the night in a "dream state" - a contact is made. Your cousin tells you of the dream.

Your initial reaction is "Why didn't she come to me?"

Please don't think your mother is angry with you and that's why she didn't come to you. It's just less upsetting for your cousin or someone else to receive a visit with a message other than you at that point. Those who have transitioned don't want to upset us. Even though you may be longing for a connection, the reality is, you may get upset. Please give it time. Your loved ones will make some type of connection with you, one way or another. In the meantime, ask about the connection to the person who had the visit with questions, such as: What did she look like? What did she say? What was she dressed like? Was she with anyone else?

We as humans tend to feel guilty when someone transitions to Heaven. The reasons are numerous. Sometimes we don't have an opportunity to say good-bye. People transition and we either didn't know about it, or we just left the hospital room, there was a car crash, a sudden heart attack, the list is endless. There may have been decisions regarding DNR (Do not resuscitate) to make regarding life support issues, organ donation, cremation vs. burial, what type of stone, where to bury them, type of casket, a suicide you feel could have been prevented, especially in the event of something so fast and unpredictable. Again, the list is endless right down to what they should wear. All these things (unless something is clearly written) weigh heavily on whoever is left behind to make decisions. If your loved ones are going to visit someone else, it is only because your heart is still hurting, and they are simply going to someone who may not get as upset as you would. That is, it. Plain and simple.

They will not come to you if they feel you will relive so to speak the experience of their transition. You may want and even crave them to come to you. It is up to them. Sometimes people have visits right away. Others will have one or two visits, and some will have more frequent ones. Some people never have a "visit" at all. Please don't be discouraged, because there are other signs to watch for.

Feel gratitude and blessed that they have found someone they can connect with to get you a little comfort. If you find you are feeling guilty about anything I previously mentioned, I ask you to please let go of feeling guilty and remember they are never mad with you if they are not coming to you. I hear it repeatedly in my world of spiritual counseling. Remember, there is no right or wrong to these experiences.

Fragrances

Afterlife people are famous for coming to us by way of the sense of smell. You may not see them, but they can let you know they are there with a favorite fragrance or scent. Some common examples are cigarettes or cigars (if they smoked), a favorite perfume, or aftershave. Cooking or baking aromas are also common, though it could be any scent or fragrance that you would associate with them. The experience of a fragrance or the aroma is often a wispy one, meaning that it doesn't linger. What is also fascinating is that not everyone in the same room will have the same experience with smelling something. See the following example. Also, these fragrant signs will present in a place where you would not normally expect them.

Here is an example. There could be several sisters sitting together and one may comment on smelling mom's perfume. The other sisters may say they don't smell anything and that the sister who commented smelling the perfume is crazy. In this instance, the mother is coming through to the one sister to let her know she is there. There may be a difficult or challenging situation going on with that one daugher. This is not an uncommon occurrence. The mom, just being mom, wants her daughter to know she is watching over her and is trying to help her from Heaven. I often have that experience with my clients. I will smell something of their loved ones and they will not. I am still not sure how those in the afterlife accomplish that, but they do. Don't think you are crazy. It happens. We are naturally creative as human beings, but I am not convinced we are that creative.

One time I channeled a man who was an auto mechanic. He left a wife and several children to go to Heaven. His entire family reported smelling automotive oil for months after he passed. It turned out he would come home after work smelling like grease. It is certainly a distinct aroma! At first, they all thought it odd. But after a while, they felt comforted by it. Even though they couldn't see or hear him, they knew he was there with them all.

Many times, people smell flowers. Here is something else to think about: not only the afterlife people can smell sweet, but most of the time our angels carry a very sweet fragrance. When I smell something sweet like roses, but even sweeter, it is typical of the Blessed Mother. I smell her and see her when there are problems or concerns involving children or if a woman is trying to conceive a child and she is worried. The Blessed Mother appears often when a woman has lost a child. It doesn't matter what the client's religion is.

Again, fragrant signs will occur in places where you wouldn't expect them to. If you don't allow smoking in your home, and suddenly one or more of you smell cigarette smoke, it's likely one of your loved ones that used to smoke and is there for a visit. If you are on a city street and suddenly smell flowers, it could be a loved one or one of your angels or even a transitioned pet. Of course, if you are at a florist, in a garden or have flowering plants in your home, naturally you would smell the flowers. Not everything is woo woo (supernatural).

A friend of mine was kind enough to share two of her experiences related to these signs.

How I met Vanessa:

Many years ago, there was an article in the Milford Citizen about Nutmeg Healing Center featuring Vanessa, who is a psychic and medium. The article intrigued me, so I decided to call and schedule an appointment with her. That was the start of this friendship. She is one of the most honest and caring people I know. Vanessa has helped me by giving me angelic guidance in many situations. My mom and husband have passed, and she has given divine messages from them many times.

My husband's passing was very fast and unexpected. I was in shock and had a very hard time for quite a while. Soon after my husband left, every time I entered my bedroom, I would smell cigarette smoke. Just to let you know, my husband was a smoker. I keep his cremated ashes in the bedroom, so I can feel close to him. I honestly couldn't understand where the smell was coming from and had mentioned the experience to quite a few people and nobody understood. I even called the funeral director and asked if it was possible to smell smoke when someone has been cremated. He said he had never heard of it and didn't think it was possible to smell cigarette smoke from an urn. I told Vanessa about it and she said he was letting me know he is still with me. Now I know he is with me every day, and it always makes me feel certain there is life after death.

Additionally, the day of my Mom's burial, my oldest son and his wife were in the kitchen of my house. They were standing in front of the sink and all of a sudden, they smelled Mom's perfume. At the same time, both of them said "Gram is here!" They immediately told me about it and mentioned how happy they were that she was watching over them.

Please remember to thank your loved ones for giving you these awesome signs and taking time to visit.

Yes! They will touch us

Don't get creeped out by this. It's more common than most people think. Many times, connections are made by our loved ones and pets touching us. You may feel a hand on your shoulder, on the upper part of your back, on the top of your hand, the top of your head or even a gentle brush stroke over one side of your face. Those in the afterlife can kiss us too. They will kiss our foreheads, cheeks, and tops of our heads. They even play with our hair.

I've seen transitioned spouses on the other side hug their spouse or partner. Parent's will hug a child. Even pets get hugged. You may be standing in front of your kitchen sink washing dishes and then suddenly feel a hug. Now you believe that you were just thinking of your mother for example, and how much you miss her. Then you go on to think you are making it up. No, you *can't* make this up. Those who have transitioned are holding or hugging you to console you and let you know they are there with you. They are also receiving your thoughts of missing them. Take a moment to say thank you in your mind or aloud for the touch.

I'd like to spend a moment here on children we never had a chance to meet. I am referring to miscarriages, abortions, and stillborn children. Let's say you are at the end of your day. You have worked, managed your daily tasks of family and life, and you finally are lying in bed about to go to sleep. Suddenly you feel a few hairs on your head being touched or "played with". You get the feeling as though there might be a little bug in your hair. After turning on the light you see nothing. There is something, and you are just not seeing it. Children we've lost love to play with Mom's hair, especially at night. They will also stroke the side of the mother's face very gently. Mothers may even see a slight depression on the side of the bed, as though someone is sitting there. I believe the children do this just when we are about to fall asleep because that is when we are finally quiet to a point and they can make a connection with us. This is neither a visit nor a dream. Please don't think you are losing your mind because it is a special moment. Experiences through my spiritual counseling practice have also shown that if you are the dad who has lost a child, the child can be a little rougher with you then with mom. If you are a man, you may feel a presence on your lap while you are sitting it could be your child.

It's common for the afterlife people to sleep next to us. I've told many people where their spouse is sleeping next to them, whether to the right or left of my client. I've heard jokes about the spouse still *here* not having to hear the snoring anymore. They may even wrap us in their arms as we sleep. It's *never* a frightening experience. My 104-year-old grandmother, Phyllis shared with me before she transitioned that her husband (my Papa) was in the bed next to her. It was very real she said. And she was surprised to see how young he was. They also had a little conversation.

I'd like to talk about touching our backs for a moment. Afterlife people will generally give us gentle nudges in our upper backs, just below our necks. They do this if we are indecisive about something and feel "stuck". Meaning we are indecisive about what to do next because of being overwhelmed. They also enjoy letting us know how proud they are of us for something just accomplished. They notice everything.

Sometimes you may feel a pressure in your lower back. I am not talking about real back pain. It will feel like a gentle pressure or a gentle nudge. Again, my experience tells me those nudges in the lower back are from your guardian angels or other angels to assist you in a situation in which you feel "stuck". Sometimes after people transition, we feel emotionally paralyzed. I haven't met one afterlife person yet that didn't want us to move forward and get either back to work or just stay connected to life. If you are feeling "stuck" for any reason and feel a very subtle pressure on either of these areas of your back, just know it can be either a missed loved one or one of your guardian angels telling you to get going.

On occasion, I've had opportunities to see an afterlife person put their hand right into the living person's heart chakra or heart center. It is in the center of the chest. Suddenly, a person feels an incredibly loving sensation that travels through their entire body. Sometimes, people will feel deep warmth coming from the top of their head also. Afterlife people send love and healing vibrations through touch to help us all the time.

Touches can include feelings of warmth, coolness, and light pressure. The sensations don't last for a long time. Like the fragrances, they are wispy and fast. I am not saying your entire body feels like it is turning into a frozen popsicle or a fiery feeling. The sensation is a little spot on your body that feels either warm or cool. They are never extreme temperature changes. I am not comparing these warm/hot sensations to hot flashes either ladies. I find Papa will gently put his hand on the top of my head if I am trying to do too much or feel overwhelmed. This always happens especially when I have a lot on my mind. I feel an incredible amount of calming and warmness travel through my entire body. A feeling of AAHHH comes over me. The feeling just reminds me he is there giving me some assurance to calm down and everything will be OK.

Sometimes we touch them and don't even know it. Most humans can't see the afterlife people and walk through them. You'll recognize this when you feel a little tingling rush through your body, or your hairs on your arms and/or the back of your neck stand up. Your spine may also tingle. If you walk somewhere and experience those feelings, now you know what it is. The good news is that they don't mind. I think they get a charge out of it. No pun intended. Well, maybe just a little pun.

Breezes

You may experience a subtle breeze pass through the room or right by you. *Pay attention.* This isn't a blast of air. Of course, if there is an air conditioner or a fan on, please remember common sense! It can be a cooler or a warmer sensation than the environment you are in. If there is no valid reason for the subtle breeze, know it's a sign and please thank whoever is with you from the afterlife.

Moving things around

Here is something peculiar to think about. Yes, they do move things around!

Afterlife people are notorious for relocating items and moving stuff around. However, they will not literally throw things around your house or work environment. *That* type of activity is not from your loved ones. If things are flying around your house, call a priest or similar type of person who can help rid your dwelling of that negative energy. Please don't call me. I prefer to connect with "lighter" energies.

Pay attention to *what* is being moved. It usually involves something meaningful to them. If your loved one was a prankster, he or she may move anything just to get a reaction.

Pictures are always one of the more common examples. Many people place pictures of loved ones (both *here* and *there*) on furniture such as an end table, coffee table, nightstand and even clusters of family pictures on walls is common. You generally know how you leave things in your home or workplace after cleaning, organizing, or rearranging. When you arrive home or wherever from the typical day's running around, for whatever reason, you notice a picture not quite as you left it. The picture may be set on a piece of furniture, shelf or even on the wall. You become aware that it is either crooked or tilted a bit. You return it to its original position. The same thing happens the next day. By now you may be blaming other people in the house for moving or futzing around with the picture. Take notice of who is in the photo. It's commonly a picture with someone in Heaven, whether he or she is in it by him- or herself or with other people. If there was a train or some other kind of rumbling that affected the house, it would make sense that all the pictures would be slightly out of alignment. But, if you straighten out the picture on the end table for example, and it goes back to being crooked again, take a moment to thank whoever is in the picture for just being around you.

I'd like to share yet another story from my life with you. My Uncle Benny was a jeweler, and unfortunately was murdered when he was forty-two at his brand-new jewelry store in East Haven, Connecticut. I was seventeen years old. My Aunt Shirlee decided to keep the store open for several years after his transition. I worked with her in the store for two years. Anyone who remembers fads from the 1970s will remember this type of decor. The office had a very thick shag rug with multiple colors of blues and greens. The store had a tropical theme with peacock colors. It was beautiful.

One day, Aunt Shirlee dropped a small pouch of loose diamonds into the shag rug in her office. We were both on our hands and knees looking for the diamonds without any luck. It was like looking for the proverbial needle in a haystack. Uncle Benny's picture was set on top of the file cabinet in the office. Aunt Shirlee was so flustered that she asked Uncle Benny to somehow let her know where the diamonds were. Immediately, the picture flew from the top of the file cabinet and landed on the rug.

Right away, my aunt said, "OK, we will find them now!"

Sure enough, we found them all clustered together just next to his picture that was now on the shag rug. Neither one of us was afraid of what happened. In fact, we were both happy. I know he was too!

Afterlife people can move other objects around as well. Most people have a routine when they come home from work. We usually drop our keys, purse and whatever we are holding in our hands in certain areas.

Here's a scenario: You placed your keys on the counter and have some things to take care of before you go out again. After running around trying to get yourself and other things in order before you leave again, you reach for your keys, and they are a little farther away from where you left them. You give it a quick thought, but that's it. You run off to your next destination. We are all very busy in these hectic times but remember the afterlife people can move things around, even keys. Don't always blame your spouse, partner, child or even the pet. It's probably someone on the other side just trying to get your attention. All I can ask is that you bring your awareness to what is being moved. Chances are you may feel like you are losing your mind, but you are not.

Electrical Connections

Afterlife people love to mess around with anything electrical. Anything electrical in your home, car, office or outside will do. Once they figure out they can play like this, they have a blast. We are electrical beings here on the planet. There is an electrical current (life force energy or chi) that runs throughout our bodies. But once we cross over into Heaven, those frequencies change, and we are even more electrical in vibration. Therefore, the afterlife people resonate very well with electrical frequencies of things you may have in your home or other electrical devices. They can connect easily with them. It can be kind of unsettling at first, but when it dissipates, in a strange way, you may find yourself almost missing it.

Those who have transitioned make their presence known through blinking lights and by disrupting remote controls, computers, garage door openers, small and large appliances, photos you take with a camera or cell phone camera as well as doorbells and cell phones. They will turn on any kind of music box or ring hanging indoor or outdoor chimes. Of course, if there is wind blowing outside and your chimes are chiming, well... remember not everything is woo-woo.

LIGHTS

They connect with one or two lights in the house and will make them blink on and off. Sometimes, light bulbs will blow out repeatedly. You can certainly have the light fixture checked out, but most likely it is fine. Of course, if all the lights in your house are blinking on and off, I would strongly advise you calling your local power company or an electrician to have everything checked. Afterlife people will not make a disco club out of your house.

REMOTE CONTROLS

When trying to change the station, the remote control is not cooperating, even after you have changed the batteries. People tend to become inpatient when something like a remote control does not cooperate. Here is what I suggest you do: Pause for a moment (you, not the remote) and take a good look at what is playing on the screen. There is usually a familiar meaning that connects with what is playing on the TV to an afterlife person you love. The scene may also have something to do with events happening in your own life.

COMPUTERS

Like remote controls, your computer may not be cooperating the way it should. It may look like it's on the fritz. So, you call the local all-night computer repair person, and nothing is wrong with it. Then voila! It starts working properly again. It could be a fluke, or it could be a connection from a loved in in Heaven. You decide!

GARAGE DOOR OPENERS

I haven't had this experience myself, but I have heard this story from some of my clients. In this scenario, typically the family is at home and hears the garage door go up, but all the family members are in the house. They check, and sure enough, the garage door is open.

On one occasion, I was on my way to present a "Messages" (group gallery reading) several years ago at a private home. People were excited about the evening. When I mentioned about the idea of garage doors going up and down for no apparent reason, they all freaked out. As it so happened, just before I arrived, the garage door opened up by itself. One of the family members closed the garage door. Soon after, it went up again. It turned out that one of the attendees had lost a child and she was playing a little prank! It didn't happen while I was at the house. The little girl was having fun and getting a reaction.

APPLIANCES

This type of sign can be very interesting. Afterlife people can affect small kitchen appliances or larger ones, such as a washer or dryer. Sometimes the appliance will turn itself on while it is already plugged in. In other instances, you may have an appliance (or another electrical device) that is *not* plugged in and it turns on. Although the latter is a little unsettling, remember that afterlife people have a very high frequency of electrical energy.

Here is a cool personal story I feel you will enjoy. A friend of mine and I took a trip to Vermont for a weekend. We were staying at my friend, Sonia's house. The house itself is very interesting because many years ago it was a small, local church. Over time, and several owners with Sonia being the most recent, the church was converted to a five-bedroom house. Sonia updated the house and even had it lifted to support a poured cement-basement. It's always filled with spirit visitors who are completely harmless. My friend chose a bedroom downstairs to sleep in and I took a bedroom upstairs. The time was about half past ten in the evening. We decided to call it a night and turn in. As I was lying in my bed upstairs I heard many kinds of music. I heard music of marching bands; rock and roll and then classical music. It was very loud. This house is in the boon docks and is very isolated. There is no high school field or outdoor area for a concert. Plus, everything that I know of in the area closes by about seven in the evening. After listening to this for a while, and being curious, I decided to get up and walk downstairs. At that point, the music completely stopped. I ventured downstairs only to find my friend standing outside of her bedroom looking panicked. Staring at her startled face, I was just about to ask her if she had heard any music, when, she asked me the same question.

Of course, I said "yes, that's why I came downstairs".

The music was coming from the next bedroom located next to my travel companion's room. There is an old arch-style radio in that bedroom for decoration. My friend said the music was coming from the old radio in the adjacent room to hers. I disagreed because I knew it was never plugged in. It was a decoration and never worked. My friend Sonia who as mentioned earlier owns the house, had told me years ago she picked it up as a decoration only and it never worked. We went into the bedroom with the radio in it together only to confirm it was *not* plugged in. To say the least, my travel companion was a little beside herself. She said she didn't want to sleep alone and asked if she could sleep with me. After telling her I liked her but not that much, I suggested she sleep in the bedroom across the hall from mine upstairs. She did, and we kept both our doors open. We didn't hear any more music after that.

A client of mine had a similar experience with appliances. Everyday her mom would enjoy a cup of tea and toast. When this client lost her mother, she acquired her mom's toaster and set in on the counter in her own kitchen. The toaster would click on quite often. The daughter would smell the toast. *Mom* is here, she would think. It was kind of comical because the toaster was never plugged in. Mom was just making herself feel at home.

It's not that common for electrical things to turn on without being plugged in, but it can happen. If it is really getting on your nerves, just ask whoever is doing these things to stop it and find another way to communicate.

CAMERAS AND PHOTOGRAPHS

We all know people are always taking pictures of just about anything these days. There are all kinds of other things that can show up in pictures, so I would like to bring your attention to some of them. The important thing is to look beyond the subject matter of the picture. If you are looking at a wedding picture, look above and around the bride and groom. This applies to any photos for that matter. Always look beyond the people in the pictures.

You may see little bubble-like shapes. They are called "orbs." They are energies that can include people from the other side or even angels. They can appear to be translucent, dense, white, different colors, small or large. They can be all alone or in clusters. I had the opportunity to see photographed pictures that were taken after 9/11. It looked like it was snowing orbs and was amazing. I could feel these were not only the people that transitioned that terrible day, but all the loved ones coming to meet them and all of God's helpers from many realms, including, of course, angels. Orbs will cluster around people, especially when there is music, happiness, joy, and love.

I also had an opportunity with my friend Kathleen to see if we could capture pictures of fairies at her farm. She had me sit on a bench where I was instructed to meditate. I invited the fairy realm to come to my side if they wished. They came. We loaded the pictures onto her computer. There were a couple of teeny, tiny orbs near my face in the photos. Upon zooming in on a couple of them, we found one to have a little boy's face in it. Another orb was quite interesting also. There was an angel's face surrounded by the twelve signs of the zodiac inside the orb. If I didn't see it myself, I don't think I would have believed it. We named her the Mosaic Angel. The interesting thing about the Mosaic Angel is that we are unable to print it. Both Kathleen and I can only view it on our computers. If you have pictures that you can zoom in on, try it. You may be very surprised to find out who is there.

Rays of light streaming from a person or around a person are also very common in a picture. The rays may appear white, but other colors are also common. They may be straight beams or rays, or they may have a swirly and smoky look. These rays will show up in pictures at any time. It can be someone's guardian angel, but it can also be an afterlife person. The next picture is of me in my back-yard. My son took this with his cell phone camera. I was getting ready to have a bonfire and was just ecstatic that he was visiting me from California. We love to have bonfires together while eating and chatting. You can see the streams of light all around. If you look closely, over my right shoulder you will see one of my angels. I have several pictures of my angels, which will be in another book. I just wanted to let you see this one because of all the activity in it. Isn't it awesome? For a more defined picture, please visit my website, heavensguide.com.

I have a photo of a friend of mine, named Lauren. It was taken many years ago when she and her husband went to Florida for a vacation. Her husband took her picture. After it was developed she was amazed at what she saw. She immediately brought that photo, along with some other photos to show me. Lauren's brother, Bill unfortunately died rather quickly several years prior to the photo being taken. Because I've connected so many times for Lauren, I feel I know Bill. He has the same birthday as my son, Shane. The next picture shows Lauren, but Bill is also present. He is seen so clearly standing behind Lauren, with his arm over her head, leaning on her. The picture is so clear. He is smiling and, if you look closely, you can see what he is wearing. He is seen with a tank top on. Why not? He was on a cruise in Florida. He also has an intense beam of light coming from his forehead up to Heaven. This is an energy cord connecting him to Heaven like an umbilical cord. It stems directly from his third eye. The third eye is our psychic center in the forehead. For a more detailed picture, please go to my website, heavensguide.com.

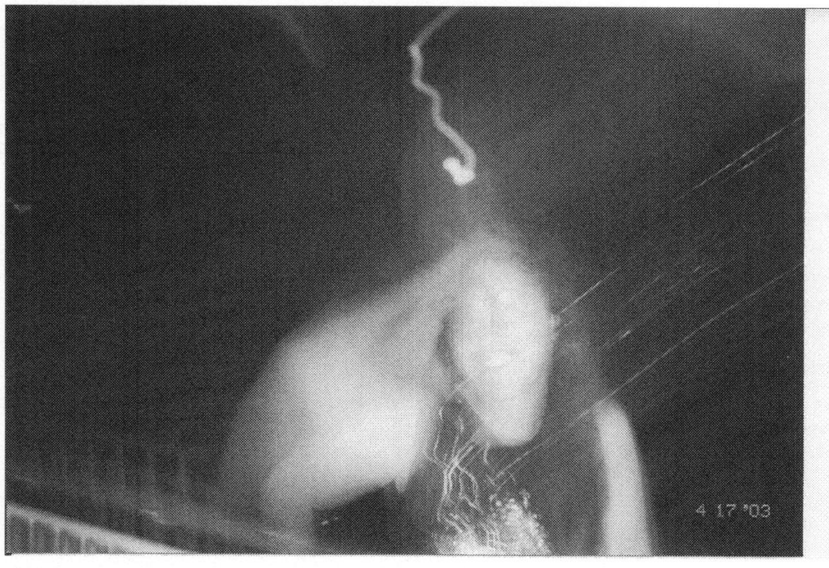

People and animals can also appear in photos that have mirrors in them, but don't forget to rule out the possibility of a flash reflection in the mirror.

This is a fascinating story about one of my client's photos. It is amazing. One of my clients lost her husband several years ago. He was sick for several years before he transitioned. She arranged for a birthday party for him about two weeks prior to him transitioning. They loved each other dearly, and still do. She came to me with some photos and asked me to look through them. My client had the pictures developed after Tom transitioned several weeks after his after his cel-ebration. They were taken at the dining table before the guests arrived. The table was decorated with lovely centerpieces. I began to look for orbs and the like but did not see any. I looked through the entire set of pictures. When I was looking at the last photo, I couldn't believe what was there. In capital, red digital letters, the phrase "I LOVE YOU" was written with digital red hearts on either side. I wanted to cry. She had showed her adult children these photos and they couldn't believe it either. I was simply amazed. Does everyone understand how fast this person had to work to have this happen? The film runs through developing machines very quickly, but, he managed to make it happen just in time.

I LOVE YOU

DOORBELLS

Ding Dong…no it's not AVON calling!

Door bells will ring in the middle of the night or at any time. If your door bell rings, you get up to check, but no one is there, it may be an afterlife person trying to get in touch with you.

Let's look at this logically for a minute. First, a burglar is not going to ring your doorbell late at night and announce they are about to rob you. If that happened, you have a very stupid and inexperienced burglar at your door. If the ringing doorbell annoys you, please just ask the afterlife person to stop ringing it late at night or anytime that it bothers you. They quickly forget the physical human body needs sleep to function properly the following day since they don't need to rest.

My Mom told me a story relating to a doorbell incident at her house. She called me one day and said the strangest thing happened. She began to tell me that my Dad was sleeping, and she was lying awake. The doorbell rang once around midnight. She got up and looked out the window, but nobody was there. After she told me the story on the phone the next morning, I "tuned" into it. Her father, Howard (my grandfather) told me it was him. My grandfather Howard, was and still is the most quiet, gentle, and polite soul. Of course, he would ring the doorbell before entering anyone's house. Mom's only response was a suspicious hum.

CELL PHONES

The latest rage is communicating through cell phones. Afterlife people can talk through the static on a cell phone. They can play around with your ringtone as well. They can reset it to a new one you are not familiar with and then revert to the one you had previously. I've had experiences with my phone ringtone as well as client's cell phone ringers being changed while in a session.

Pay special attention to *my* next cell phone story. A lot of people are experiencing this but may think it is a problem with the phone. One of my uncles transitioned suddenly in August of 2006 even though he had cancer for quite a while. He was given a prognosis of six months just one week prior to his transition. My son and I went to the hospital to visit him on Thursday evening. The following morning, we received a call he had transitioned around eight in the morning. I was at a deli later in the afternoon picking up eggplant along with sausage and pepper trays to bring over to my cousin's house. While at the deli, I was speaking to my cousin (his daughter). During the conversation, my cell phone went dead. The battery was charged, and the signal was strong, yet there was no connection or, so it seemed. Excusing myself, I went outside to call my cousin back. I had no luck. Suddenly, I heard a lot of static coming from my phone as I was trying to call her. It was loud and reminded me of an old ham radio. In between the static I heard a very raspy voice say, "I'm OK". It was my Uncle on the phone! I closed the flip cell phone and said out loud, "So that's what that was about. I'll let them know."

I proceeded to my cousin's house with the food. Upon having a conversation with my cousin, she expressed to me that for almost thirty minutes she couldn't figure out why we couldn't reach each other. My uncle is too funny. He was interfering with both our phones. Since she was feeling overwhelmed with planning, she wasn't tuned in to her father communicating with her. I bring this to your attention because it is happening on a more frequent basis. Needing to learn to listen to the not-so obvious is so important.

LAND LINE PHONES

People on the other side will also connect with us through land line phones. When they call, there is no sound as if nobody is on the other the end. It is an eerie silence. When you check the caller ID, it reads out of area, unknown or something similar. When I had a land line for my business phone, this would happen frequently throughout the day. I would joke around and tell them to come back when their loved ones are with me for a session. If this happens to you on occasion or frequently, you will usually have a feeling about who it is. I like to kid around, but who do you call? 1-800-CALLGOD? What do you say? "I know my mother just called, can you get her back on the phone?"

While staying with my friend Lenore, in Tennessee, we had a cool landline experience. Lenore's husband, Paul had transitioned. I had the pleasure of meeting him while he was *here*. He unfortunately had cancer and transitioned from it. Paul was *never* a believer in anything spiritual. Lenore, on the other hand, is very gifted and spiritual herself. She was always trying to convince and enlighten him spiritually. She took very good care of him until he transitioned to Heaven. Since he left, he has given numerous signs. Lenore and Paul were originally from Brooklyn, New York. She moved to Tennessee after he transitioned so she could be with family. When I was stayed with Lenore in June 2012, the phone rang one evening. Here is how the conversation went.

She answered the phone in her New York accent "Hello…"

"Hello…"

"Hello…is anybody there?"

She heard static and quickly passed the phone to me. Even with a keen sense of listening, I heard nothing but static. She ran to shut the TV off, thinking there was too much background noise for us to hear him. The phone clicked off and the call was gone. We checked the caller ID, it read "Directory Assistance – New York". Did we have a good laugh? Yes.

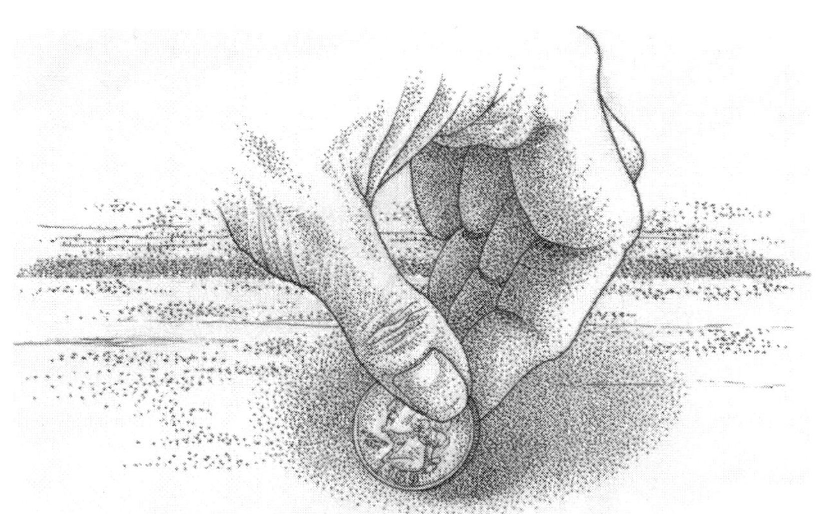

They Send Money!

Pennies from Heaven!!

Unbelievably, the afterlife people send us money. My experience is that it isn't lots of money but rather a consistency in coin type. I am still waiting for large green bills! Typically, you will either find all pennies, nickels, dimes, or quarters that turn up in the strangest places sometimes. For example, I had just thoroughly cleaned my house. After vacuuming, there is a dime sitting on the carpet. Papa is always sending me dimes. I always make it a point to save them. I purchased a couple of crystal heart shaped small jewelry dishes to keep them in, and they are filled. Saving the dimes is important to me because I feel they are presents from Pap in Heaven.

Several years ago, I was asked to participate in a spiritual show on a local cable Channel in West Hartford, Connecticut. As I approached the chair I was to sit in, I noticed there was a dime on the seat.

I smiled and said, "Thank You" aloud.

I pointed this out to the host of the New Age show. She smiled too and knew just what it meant. She may not have known who it was from, but she did know it was from someone significant.

At another time, I was missing my Grandfather and asked him where he'd been lately. I had a lot going on in my own life and was too preoccupied to feel him around. A woman came to my studio for a reading. She sat across from me for the session. The session ended, and I walked her to the door to let her out. I had a little chair by the door.

Her eyes fell upon the chair and she reached toward the chair as she said, "Oh look, a dime!"

I quickly responded, "No, don't touch it!"

Positive she thought I was insane, I decided to tell her it was a gift from my grandfather. I explained he sends me dimes, and I had just asked him where he'd been recently. During the reading, he manifested the dime for me. To this day, I really don't know how they produce tangible objects through dimensions, but they do.

On another occasion I was getting ready to leave for Vermont to work on this book. Just before leaving from Connecticut to Vermont I found two dimes in random places, so I knew Papa was around. When I arrived at the house in Vermont and got settled in, I decided to fix a little dinner for myself. Sonia kept a little evergreen tree shaped trivet on the stove. I placed my dinner on it while it cooled. I moved the trivet from one side of the stove to the other before taking my dinner off it to eat. When I got up the next morning to put the kettle on for tea, guess what was lying in the middle of the trivet? A dime! I know it wasn't there the night before. Naturally I smiled and thanked Papa for being there *again*.

I am including this next story because of the differential from the previous one. This one is about a man named Don, who was a retired police officer in Connecticut and he was just a lovely soul. I had the honor and pleasure of meeting Don before he transitioned. He and his family shared his money story with me. He told me one night he was in his underwear, walking down a hallway in his house. The thought of this man in his underwear had the family in giggles. Too much information! At a certain point, thirty-five cents (one quarter and one dime) fell from his boxers onto the floor. He thought it very odd and picked up the change. He placed it on his dresser. The next day the thirty-five cents went missing. About a week or so later, his son was visiting him. His son heard change drop. He looked down and there were thirty-five cents. It turned out his son found the money in the exact spot it had dropped from Don's boxers. I was a little perplexed about the whole thing, not just because of the thirty-five cents, but also because there was no explanation as to where it came from. Don had no idea either. Just like the English language, there is always an exception to the rule. In this case, he received a quarter and a dime, but the consistency was there. That is the first story of its kind that I've heard of.

Feathers

Keep an eye out for feathers as they can a sign of the afterlife people. Whenever I find feathers, I save them. I have several sealed sandwich bags full. Please don't get the impression I am a pack rat, I am not. These are important signs to me. I should mention that I had an umbrella cockatoo exotic bird. Her name was Luna, nicknamed Sweetie. She was beautiful and smart. Her feathers were white with a little yellow under her wings. I knew her feathers. I've been finding feathers for years before Sweetie came into my life and many since she left me for Heaven in June 2017, she was only fifteen.

One day just before I moved my business location, I was in the process of making some major changes and decisions. All of it was preoccupying me to a point. I had a couple of readings scheduled, and I had to prepare myself for them, which meant getting into the correct mind-set. I asked for help from my angels. When I arrived at work, just in front of the door was the largest white feather I'd received there in eight years. There were always plenty of pigeons around that area, but they were grey. This was a long, twilled, white feather. It was stunning. I smiled graciously and thanked the angels and whoever else was kind enough to send me that sign. I felt an immediate sense of well-being and relief. I was then able to switch gears into reading mode, and the rest of the day was fine. I also knew from that sign that my choices were goo and that everything would be fine. That was the last feather I received from my original Milford, Connecticut location. Needless to say, I added it to my collection.

Feathers can be from people on the other side, or they can be from angels. We haven't talked too much at this point about angels. If you have down bedding or anything in your house stuffed with feathers, there could be a good chance it came from the bedding or a bird if you have one. However, I will maintain if you are finding feathers in strange places or in places you just tidied up, there is a good chance it is a present from Heaven. Save these gifts if you wish.

My uncle (the cell phone uncle) comes to one of my relatives by placing long brown feathers with black dots on them in his house. They are usually in the middle of the floor in his bedroom. There is absolutely no way a bird has been in the house. These feathers appear when he has a lot going on. I believe it is my uncle just letting him know he is being watched over.

Flowers (not fragrances)

When there isn't a logical explanation of an item, including flowers brought to your attention, please consider it a sign from the afterlife. This is a rose petal story. In the year, 2000 some of my friends and I attended an all-day event at Madison Square Garden in New York City. Out of the four popular guests, two were mediums. While one of the mediums was reading for the audience, a rose petal gently floated down from the ceiling. The rose petal fell just next to the woman that was being "read." It sounded like everyone gasped in the audience. If you have ever been to Madison Square Garden, the ceiling is all rafters. Nobody in their right mind would climb up, drop a rose petal, and have that great of an aim to have it drop to the woman being "read". The entire audience was in silent amazement.

Making that special appearance!

Some people are gifted with being clairvoyant. This means they have the ability of psychic sight. I hear so often from people "*here*" they want to see someone they lost to Heaven. Most people do not see them. If you have had an experience seeing afterlife people, feel very blessed. You may only experience it one time. You may never see them at all, and that's OK too. Those that have transitioned don't show themselves to most of us because we are not ready to see them.

Think about this. You are lying in your room fast asleep, and something prompts you to wake up. You see a person hovering over or around you. Do you think you would really want to sit up, smile and have a conversation? No. You probably would initially be frightened half to death. They won't give us anything we can't handle. People on the other side that know and love us will never try to frighten us.

Several years ago, I remodeled the lower level of my house. I was finally at the stage of painting the walls, which I love doing. I was painting the room turquoise (I am not afraid to use colors my walls), when I felt like I was being watched. I looked to my right and there was a short man who was kind and very curious as to what I was doing. He looked to be in his sixties. Not saying a word, he just stood there looking at me and the color on the wall. I felt that he was happy I'd made the changes to that level of the house, but he wasn't too keen on the color. I told him out loud not to worry and I always pull things together! It will be fine. He then vanished. That was in 2004. I didn't see him again until 2010, when I was attempting to plant a garden. He was standing in the doorway of my kitchen just watching me outside in the garden. Again, I told him it would be OK, and he vanished. Since those are the only two times he has let himself be seen, I'm assuming he is OK with the rest of what I've done to the house. I believe he was the original owner who also made many changes to this little house. He just wanted me to know he was around watching.

Seeing a loved one's face in the crowd

People have reported seeing their loved ones' faces from the other side appearing in a crowded place of living people. Afterlife people have the ability to super impose a likeness of their image onto other people here, especially if they think you will see them. As you really look at the person in the crowd, you realize it isn't the person on the other side, but for that moment, you saw your loved one. Please don't think you didn't see what you did. They simply wish you to know they are nearby. Occasionally, I'm told when giving a medium reading to a client, that I take on the appearance of a loved one or present a distinct expression or mannerism of the person who has transitioned.

Did you see that?

Most of us have had the following experience: All of a sudden, you see something fly quickly in your peripheral vision. It was a little black streak out of the corner of your eye. You turn your head, but you don't see anything. You can bet that this is one of your loved ones. Although afterlife people show themselves to me with a body so I can connect them to a family member or friend, the reality is we shed our physical body at the time of the transition. Because of that, those who have transitioned can move extremely fast. We think we are zooming around these days, but we don't hold a candle to how fast afterlife people can move from place to place, and from dimension to dimension. If you see a brief shadowy energy in your peripheral vision, it means your loved one is just trying to catch your attention. Usually, after a brief shake of your head, you go about your business and forget all about it. However, if you are seeing a lot of different shining lights or other odd things that are not "normal," please make an appointment to see your eye doctor!

Can You Hear Me now?

This falls under the category of clairaudience, which is the gift of psychic hearing. Afterlife people are always talking to us, but not everyone can hear them. In my readings, they often tell me to let my client know they whisper to them. My clients almost always acknowledge the experience of hearing whispers. I recommend to clients that they be quiet when this occurs. This way they will be able to hear them better and understand the communication. Sometimes our loved ones call out our names. You may hear just one word or a bunch of words. If you hear someone from the other side, don't be frightened. Be glad you have the ability for that type of connection.

After my uncle transitioned, he communicated very clearly to me on the very night he passed. This is what happened the evening of the cell phone incident. Some insight to my uncle's personality is that my uncle was a lot of fun and was loved by many people. He made everyone laugh and was very free-spirited in his own way. He loved to play the daily and weekly lotto numbers. The Friday he transitioned, he was in room number 402 in a major hospital in New Haven, Connecticut. Please for the sake of this story, remember the hospital room number. Later that evening I was waiting for Shane to come home. At that time, I normally didn't go to bed until I knew he was either on his way home or was home. This night, Shane called me and said he was on his way home. It was about half past two in the morning. I relocated from the sofa in the living room into my bedroom where I laid down with my dog. I was facing to the right, still awake, but starting the process of winding down into a twilight sleep. All of a sudden, I heard a raspy voice again, but it wasn't in the cell phone this time.

I heard, "I'm over here" loud and clear.

Not seeing him because I was facing the other direction to where he was standing, I nearly jumped out of my skin. The dog jumped, and he was looking directly at the spot I heard the loud voice. Well, guess who? It was my uncle. And guess what time it was? 2:40 AM. Remember he passed in room number 402? They are the same numbers switched around. Only he would do that, but I told him to never do that again because he scared the dog too.

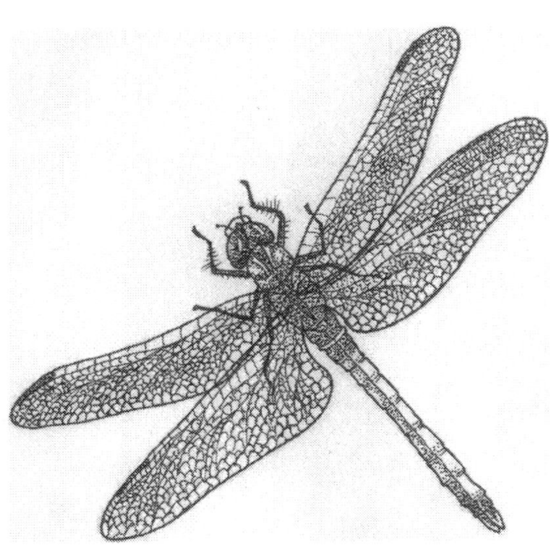

Birds, Butterflies, and Dragonflies

Seeing a bird that doesn't normally live in your yard is another common sign from Heaven. It could be a cardinal, blue bird, hummingbird, owl, hawk or just about any other kind of bird that you do not normally see. The bird appears after someone transitions. Based on my Christian background, I believe the bird is sent just as a sign. It is not actually your loved one. Someone with eastern philosophy may think otherwise.

Random pictures of birds are also signs from them. Let's say you are out shopping, looking through merchandise that has nothing to do with birds. Suddenly, you find something relating to or having a picture of a bird. Please remember you have been guided to see this as a reminder from them.

Butterflies and dragonflies are also signs from Heaven. However, they may not be always associated with afterlife people. These magical creatures are from the fairy realm and may be sent to remind you that you have the support of that realm as well. Of course, if you have a butterfly bush, expecting butterflies to be around is a given.

A neat story I want share happened several years ago at one my "Messages." I channeled a woman's mother for her. Apparently, just after the funeral service, everyone had gone to the daughter's house for a gathering. The daughter looked out her kitchen window and there was a beautiful white owl perched on the railing of the porch. Others witnessed this gorgeous creature as well. This was the only time she had ever seen it. She asked me if it meant anything. I smiled and offered comfort to her.

"You bet," I replied.

First, owls are not usually seen during the day. Since this particular bird was white, my interpretation was that it was from Heaven, which, of course, is where her mother was. Owls also have night vision. This owl was guided to the daughter to let her know that her mom could see everyone now and that she was all right. They never saw the owl again.

After my uncle (the cell phone uncle again) transitioned, for a couple of months, I kept seeing a pair of lovely, mourning doves around me every time I would think of him. Not only are they lovely birds, but people affiliate them with the Holy Spirit. I already knew he was in Heaven, but I really enjoyed seeing the birds to remind me.

One day, Shane was standing outside on our front stoop not too long after my uncle transitioned. One little dove kept flying around him and was trying to land on him. I thought it was the funniest thing. Between my uncle's playful side and my son's annoyance with trying to shoo the bird away, it was hysterical. The dove finally gave up and flew away. My son thought it was so odd. I knew it was my uncle pushing the dove to Shane. So, if you see a butterfly or a dragonfly, in a city area for example, just smile and thank who you think it is. You will see these delightful winged ones when and where you least expect it. It's just beautiful.

The butterflies you will see are usually very big and bright. Typically, they are monarch butterflies, but they can be small and brightly colored as well. This does not include moths. You may see them several times in one day or over a period of several days. They have been known to land on someone's head or shoulder. It is truly amazing.

Years ago, I was invited to present a "Messages" to mainly connect with a husband/father of a family that lived in Fairfield County, Connecticut. They typically did not observe hawks in the wife/mom's yard. They told me when they all gather together at this house; a single hawk will circle over them. It happened the day of their dad's funeral and occurred at other family gatherings. This doesn't happen when they are apart. They all acknowledged that. Their father was a very strong man, both physically and emotionally and was extremely well liked in the community, so it doesn't surprise me he picked a hawk to represent himself at family gatherings.

License Plates

Keep your eye out for license plate signs. These are common signs from Heaven. If your eyes fall randomly on a license plate that has a birthday number, another number having any meaning regarding a loved one on the other side, or their name is spelled phonetically, this is no accident. There are no coincidences. People ask me if they should play the number on the license plate. You can if you wish but seeing that doesn't automatically mean you will win. Please don't drive and intentionally look at license plates. You could have an accident. The afterlife people very hard to coordinate a car with a meaningful license plate in our path.

One night as I was driving to another group "Messages" and I found myself behind an old beat-up white and brown station wagon. The kind of station wagon you might have seen from the TV series The Mod Squad from years ago. The license plate read "DAD". I know it wasn't for me because my own father is alive. After a short time after the "Messages" began, I realized all the attending guests had lost their fathers. They were all probably in the station wagon ahead of me, so they could arrive first. If you find yourself having a connection to a license plate, just smile and say thanks.

Music and Songs

Many people have special songs that they have declared "their song". When you hear "your song," it is no accident. Your loved one is sending a clear message that he or she is nearby. If you hear a song referencing angels, it could be a person on the other side, but most likely it is one of your guardian angels. You may hear the song only once after not hearing it for a very long time, or you may hear the song many times in one day. You could hear it while getting ready for work, on the way to work, after work, or just before bed! You may hear the song several days in a row. Pay attention to all these possible scenarios because it is absolutely no coincidence you are hearing these songs.

My friend Cheryl was very good friends with a popular disco singer who is now in Heaven. The singer's name was Vickie Sue Robinson, and "Turn the Beat Around" was a big hit song of hers. It was from the 1970s. Cheryl misses her dearly and talks frequently of the wonderful friendship and great times they shared. This hit song plays at the oddest times for Cheryl.

One time, Cheryl went to the store to buy yours truly a birthday card. She was having the hardest time picking one out. A small child in the store was fussing while the child's mom was deciding on a greeting card. Cheryl was having a hard time focusing on which card to purchase because of the disruption. She finally decided on one but was drawn towards another section of the card aisle. Suddenly, a card popped out and fell to the floor. When Cheryl picked it up, read it, then opened it, she knew she had to buy it for me. It was a musical birthday card that played "Turn the Beat Around." She was so excited to know the card existed. She bought two of them: one for her and one for me. I've channeled Vicki for Cheryl several times so there is a connection between all three of us. I love opening the card from time to time, as it brings a smile to my face and joy to my heart.

Animals and Pets

Did you know pets and animals go to Heaven also?

All animals go to Heaven and pets give us signs from the other side. Primarily talking about pets, I've seen from the other side that one of your family members will always take care of your pet(s) on the other side until you arrive in Heaven. The loved one will do this even if he or she wasn't too fond of animals. This whole concept often surprises people.

I need you to understand that your pets are not floating around intergalactically in outer space somewhere. When you get to Heaven, not only will you see them, but you will get them all back. They always come to me youthful and happy. They are with us all the time, just like humans who have transitioned. The interesting point of animals is that not only do they go to their human family, but they also reunite with their biological animal family in Heaven.

They can be heard and felt just as humans on the other side. I hear transitioned animals in English. I have had the pleasure of connecting with common house pets, such as cats, dogs, and birds but also goldfish, ferrets, horses, cows, snakes, and lizards, just to name a few. If you had a cat that normally would walk between and around your feet as you were walking, they still do that. Let's say you almost trip on your way to the bathroom in the middle of the night: it is highly likely to be the afterlife cat. You need to tell the cat, in this case, that since you can't see them anymore, they need to get out of your way, so you don't fall. Pets understand you. Also, animals in Heaven visit animals that are *here*. You will notice your animals *here* look up, around and sometimes even swat at them. They can see your animals in Heaven.

Euthanizing an animal

This is such a hard choice to make. If you have had to "put down" an animal, I have never seen an animal that has crossed over angry. In fact, the animal is relieved. By this time, they are in so much pain or exhausted. Since they are unconditional in their love, they want to stay here until the bitter end for us. Our pets worry about us, protect us and always love us, no matter what. They don't spend time very much talking to me about their illnesses. Our pets are happy and relieved when they get to Heaven.

If you have an animal that transitioned suddenly for any reason, please know in your heart that your family members on the other side are always there to meet your pet. Your "babies" are never alone.

One More Point on the Animals

If you have a loved one who has transitioned and was an owner of an animal(s) that is still alive, please tell the animal who is *here* that his or her owner has transitioned and has gone to Heaven. Please tell the animal "When you see Daddy, (for example), you may see him walk through a wall or glide just above the floor. Daddy won't be feeding you anymore the way he used to, but you will still see him". They just need to be told and made aware of the situation, just as we would tell our children. It's important they understand what has happened. Animals always understand what we are saying, even though we don't always understand them.

My parents had two shelties, Heather, and Sailor. Heather transitioned. Towards the end, she (like many animals) became incontinent. My folks crated her sometimes during the daytime, but always crated her at night to sleep. Eventually some of her organs began shutting down, and it was too much for her, so my folks put her down. Both of my parents were devastated, but my Dad was very sad about the whole thing. She was a part of the family for many years. Afterwards, my Mom was telling me that Sailor would just sit and stare at Heather's crate. This went on day after day. I asked Mom if she explained to Sailor that Heather was in Heaven and he can now see her in a different way. My mother was skeptical, but finally had the little talk with Sailor. She reported soon after that he stopped sitting and staring at Heather's crate.

I've lost several pets over time and each one of them naturally had a different personality and special connection to me, just as you do with your animals. This is the story of my rescue bird named Ziggy. I acquired Ziggy, a blue headed conure parrot in early 2001. Ziggy was a hot mess when he came to me. That poor bird was undernourished, sick with infections, very angry and mean. The veterinarian estimated

Ziggy to be about twenty years old. Because he was badly neglected the poor bird had developed respiratory problems and soft nostrils that had become infected. This awesome little bird had been passed around from household to household with the last owner never cleaning his cage, let alone going to the veterinarian. He was left alone in another room, having virtually no contact with humans. When I acquired him, I immediately took him to my veterinarian in the dirty cage since I couldn't hold him without getting chewed up. The veterinarian was appalled and right away gave Ziggy vitamins and antibiotics. I asked him to do what he needed to do, and I would do what I knew how to do which was love, feed, pray and channel energy for this little guy.

I returned a month later to the veterinarian with Ziggy looking somewhat like a new bird. This so pleased the veterinarian. I remember him saying "this bird thinks he died and went to Heaven."

I threw away the old cage and bought a new one and took really good care of Ziggy. We became very close. I was the only one who could go near him, but that was major progress. He was so smart. He loved Dum Dum lollipops, pasta (he had always been with Italian families) and had quite an eclectic diet. For some reason, he didn't know he could fly. At one point, I taught him to sing almost the entire first verse of "Jingle Bells". Ziggy had learned it so well that I was going to film him and send the tape to one of the animal video shows, but his fate took him away from me March 17, 2002.

He suffered with an aneurysm in his brain. It was a horrible death to witness and not be able to do anything about it was even worse. It was too upsetting to begin to describe, but I can tell you I held him until he stopped screaming and his lifeless little body lay in my hands. Almost immediately, I saw him on the other side. He looked very much alive and in no pain. What I saw him doing was flapping his wings. He was flying! Since he didn't fly when he was *here*, he didn't know what to do with himself over *there*. At first, I got upset, because I witnessed this whole process with Ziggy and knew I could do nothing to stop it. Then I realized he needed immediate help. He didn't just need someone to watch over him. He needed someone who knew about all kinds of animals, to help him realize what he was doing was perfectly fine. I immediately called upon my maternal grandmother, Nanny. Her real name is Mary. Growing up it seemed that Nanny had about fifty thousand different kinds of animals. She also had ten children. Sometimes, I used to think she like animals more than people. When I called to her, I asked her take care of Ziggy until I could get there someday. I told her he has "issues" but is a good hearted-little fella. He just had a rough time of it *here*. All of a sudden, I saw a beautiful white light. She called his name and he flew towards the light. Her arm reached from the light and scooped up Ziggy. Seeing Ziggy with Nanny was so comforting to me. When I would walk into the house when Ziggy was *here*, I would call out his name loudly "Ziggy". He would shout "Zig-gy" with a pause between the "g" sounds. Even though it's been many years, I still hear him saying "Zig–gy. While my other bird, Sweetie was *here*, I used Ziggy's cage for traveling. I'm sure Ziggy wasn't too thrilled with sharing it. I knew he wasn't too fond of Sweetie at all. He thought of her as a prima donna. Now they are together in Heaven, along with my other birds and animals. Nanny has her hands full.

Suicide

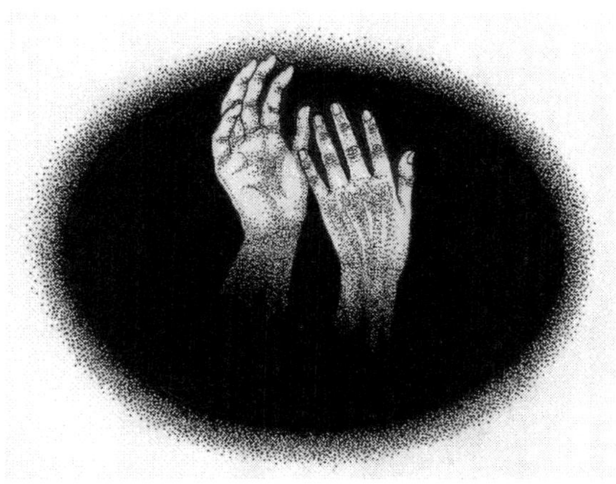

This chapter is a somber one. I was hesitant to include it, but the Heaven's Guide team of angels insisted. It is included because the suicide rates are increasing at an alarming rate around the globe. Economic instability, health, planetary shifts, broken families, as well as alcohol/drugs all contribute to people being more emotionally fragile now more than ever. So many people are feeling a severe sense of hopelessness. Coupled with those factors, the "veil" which is energy that separates our existence to other dimensions is thinning. The thinning of the veil is allowing lower frequencies of energy to affect humans and animals more intensely at this time. This all translates into lower, darker energies taking control therefore affecting people to take their own lives. I have never channeled so many people that have taken their own lives as much as the past few years. Alarmingly, it is affecting men, women, young adults and teenagers. Throughout this chapter you will read commonly asked questions about suicide.

What Happens to Someone's Soul Who Committed Suicide?

This is one of the most commonly asked questions regarding this topic. It is very important for me to have you understand this: afterlife people and GOD are aware of an individual contemplating the thought of suicide.

People who have committed suicide go to Heaven. They arrive in the lower levels first. Please rest assured that family and friends are *there* to meet them as well as angels and God. In all levels of Heaven, we review our life, even the lower levels. The review is processed with the person's teams of "mentoring" angels, people on the other side and, of course, GOD. This can be a slow process or a long process, but keep in mind, Heaven does not calculate time as we do. Processing is similar to viewing the person's life and going through each step to determine what lessons could have been dealt with differently.

Most often those who survive feel responsible in some way for not being able to prevent the act of suicide. Help is always available these days, but people don't always reach for it. Those that don't reach out are the ones that may end up taking their lives. Although it is difficult for most people to understand, suicidal people are in such dark emotional places, and they can't always see their way out of the darkness. I have channeled many folks that have chosen to end their lives. When I communicate with them, rarely do they tell me that they were immediately relieved and happy with their decision. In saying that, it is not easy for them to leave loved ones behind.

There are lots of dynamics spiritually around this. To understand the concept more easily, refer back to the Heavenly Ladder diagram.

These folks will enter levels two or three. Their mentoring teams of angels will guide them there. While they are they, they review their life on Earth and determine how to get back on track with their soul's journey. They may not be as high up initially on the spiritual ladder but remember at least they are in Heaven. While they are working on their own spiritual path, they can also visit their loved ones in Heaven. It is an abstract concept.

How Can We Help People Who Have Taken Their Life?

Prayers, prayers and more prayers. Prayers always elevate a person's soul or (vibration). Prayers don't have to be said in a place of worship: they can be offered anywhere and anytime. For example, you can pray sitting at your kitchen table with a cup of tea or coffee or even driving your car. Asking to help the person on the other side is always heard by God. You can light a candle in a place of worship or at home and ask for God and the angels to help that soul along their spiritual journey in Heaven. If you know of someone who has taken their life or hear of someone you didn't know through the news or even in a conversation, I urge you to send those folks light, love and clarity. The goal is to raise their vibration, so they reach their full spiritual potential. Prayers to the entire surviving family help in a special way also.

While it takes people out of their immediate physical situation of distress, it doesn't alleviate the problems experienced. It is in Heaven that people have an opportunity to also see the impact of their decision to themselves *and the survivors.* The same rule applies to accidental deaths from drug and alcohol overdoses. These afterlife people are always apologetic to those they left behind.

I had an opportunity to give a young man about thirty years old a reading. This young fella had some serious challenges taking place in his life. He was very attractive and smart. But, he had no self-esteem.

Blessed with two little girls whom he loved dearly, he had their names tattooed on his arm. Having difficulties with the mother of the children and a lack of steady employment, he fell into an emotionally dark place. He didn't want to move back in with his parents and be a burden to them despite their open invitation and love for him. A year or so went by when I received a call from his sister to set an appointment for a reading for herself and her mother. As soon as it became apparent that he was on the other side, I was heartbroken for both he and his family. This young man (whom I'd seen so much potential for) took his own life just before Christmas of that year. He had lost his job and couldn't buy his little girls Christmas gifts. He checked into a local motel and hanged himself. Family, friends, and acquaintances were all devastated. When he talked to me from the other side, he explained he was so upset with the "bitch," as he referred to the mother of his two little girls. He went on to explain to me he would never let anyone get the best of him to the point where he would take his own life again. Of course, he was OK in Heaven, but, he had absolutely no idea of the pain he would witness from Heaven, seeing his girls, his mother, sister and so many more negatively affected by his actions. Everyone loved him dearly and unconditionally and would have helped him if he allowed it. He had a wonderful support system but just couldn't see his way out. It was such a loss.

Another one of my clients came with her brother for a reading. He was extremely depressed. He explained to me he was extremely financially successful, but, with the downturn in the economy, he ended up losing all his money while working in the mortgage-lending business. Many people he approved mortgages for had lost their homes. To him, his situation was hopeless. He had a beautiful wife and two little children. During the course of the reading, I forecasted an upcoming job opportunity in New York City for him. I told him everything would be OK in the not too distant future. He had attempted suicide about three months prior to the reading. He assured his sister he would never try that again. I sensed psychically that he might try to do it again, and he assured me he wouldn't do that. I joked that it wouldn't be pretty because he would get an earful from me if I had to talk to him in Heaven, especially since I told him things would be fine. He did smile, but his self-esteem was so low, and his guilt was hanging heavily over him. His sister had dedicated her own life to him for over a year in order to help him get through the darkest period in his life. She stepped in where his wife couldn't. His wife didn't know what to do with him or how to handle the situation. The angels were thankful to the sister for her dedication.

In January 2009 I received a frantic phone call from his sister. My heart sank. Her brother had succeeded in hanging himself in the backyard of his house while the children were off at school and his wife was at work. No one could figure out why. He was, in fact about to start the job in New York that I had predicted. In every way, he was on the road to success and recovery. This broken man was in such a dark place and was overcome with a desire not to be on this plane anymore. His confidence and self-esteem were so eroded, that he still couldn't see his way out of his own darkness. I had two opportunities to connect with him. One time was with his widow and the next time with his beloved sister. I kept my promise and gave him an earful. He decided he wasn't in a better place after all. It's not that Heaven isn't a wonderful place, but now he was able to see all the pain his decision caused to his loved ones he left behind. Perhaps that is hell.

If you are or know of someone thinking of suicide, *please* reach out for help. Even though things feel so desperate at times, there is always help. There are 1-800 suicide phone lines available, psychotherapy, medical doctors and even medications. Between the obvious challenges everyone faces in our lives and the darkness prevailing all around us right now, people need to understand there are options, even if it feels hopeless. The repercussions of suicide to everyone left behind are just devastating. Parents, siblings, children, friends, coworkers, acquaintances will all feel guilty that either they didn't see it coming, ignored the signs or just could have helped somehow. The people taking their own lives don't know they will witness the pain they caused to all they left behind. They will witness the anguish and pain their family and friends are experiencing forever.

Suicide is not an escape. I can't tell you how many times I have heard from someone who ended his or her own life express many repeated apologies to everyone they knew. I have never run across anyone on the other side that was really glad they took their life. There are always re-grets and eternity can be a very long time. Unfortunately, I fear we will witness more and more of this dark energy in the next several years to come with the economy the way it is, and people's feelings of hopeless-ness, not just in the United States, but worldwide.

There is always help. Not only from Heaven, but here on Earth too. It's important for us and the people in Heaven that families and friends stick together and honor them. Say prayers. Get involved with public awareness on the matter. Plant a tree, grow a garden, eat a cupcake, or do something fun for them in their honor. Always be grateful for the experience of loving that very special person. Know they are in God's hands and there is no better place to be.

The Last Chapter

I was trying to decide if I should call this last chapter of the book "The Last Chapter" or "The First Chapter". My angels and guides thankfully recommended I call it "The Last Chapter." I wrestled with the title because depending on how we think of it, transition can be considered either the last or first chapter of life.

I am dedicating this chapter to my late cousin, Mark. I used to call him Marky when we were children. "Cousin Marky" to be exact. Mark was diagnosed with diabetes when he was sixteen. He never took good care of himself throughout the years, despite his apparent invincibility. He went on to marry and have two daughters. On January 3, 2009, he was found dead in his bed by his then ex-wife and his two girls. He had been quite sick for a long period of time and had experienced major complications from the diabetes, including loss of extremities, eye problems and some other things. It was hard for him to get around. An autopsy wasn't performed, but I feel he had a heart attack when he transitioned. He was forty-seven.

On January 3, 2009 a friend of mine from New York City came into town for a girl's night. Our agenda for the evening was to each get a massage, have a reflexology session and then go somewhere to dinner.

As it turned out, the massage therapist cancelled at the last minute, and I called at least ten others see if I could find a replacement. Not one was available. I understand very well that everything happens for a reason, but sometimes things can be a little frustrating. The plan was going to be that while one of us had a massage, the other would have a reflexology session, and then we would switch. My plans went right out the window when I couldn't find a massage therapist that would come to the rescue.

I picked up my friend from the train station and took her to my studio in Milford, Connecticut. Since we didn't have a massage therapist, I had my reflexology first while she waited. When it was her turn, I decided to wait in my other treatment room (where I did readings) in my nice, big, easy chair while my friend had her feet "squeezed" as she calls it. I did a little meditation for myself since I had a "free" hour.

I began meditating and slowly drifting off, enjoying my relaxation. All of a sudden, my maternal grandmother, Mary (the one who loves animals) was standing in front of me. She so politely presented a birthday cake with candles on it. I then saw a lot of my maternal family members, including my mom's father, Howard, who rarely appears to me from Heaven. I noticed my Aunt Lillian, Uncle David and many others.

"OK" I began thinking, *there goes my relaxing meditation*!

I thought at first, "Oh how nice is this? They are here to send me off with a birthday wish". After all, in February I was turning the big "Five Oh". However, that wasn't the case either. There arrival was two-fold. They were partly wishing me a happy birthday.

Nanny kept repeating "January third, January third." "Call your mother."

Now, that I knew what to do, it suddenly occurred to me that they were all waiting to pick someone up to carry into Heaven.

My first words to Nanny were "Are you here for me?"

"No" she replied.

There was a brief relief since I didn't finish the book yet and I have too many things still to do here on the plane. My thoughts raced towards my mom.

"Are you here to pick up Mommy?" I asked.

"No. Just call your mother and mention January third."

"OK" I said, "I will do that right now."

My grandmother and grandfather reminded how much they loved me. My quiet grandfather piped up and said, "I will help you with your book."

I was stunned. He reminded me that he was an editor. He worked through the Great Depression as an editor. I had forgotten all about that. He also was sick when I was a teenager, but I remember he always worked and was a great money manager. Just after the "family visit," I quickly snapped out of what was my meditation turned channeling and called Mom. Luckily, she picked up the phone. I explained my experience to her and nothing about it made sense to her. Nanny's birthday was in January but wasn't until later in the month. She transitioned in February, so January third wasn't making any sense at all. Mom and I talked while my friend's feet were still being "squeezed". Mom thought my experience with the "family visit" sounded fun and interesting, but we both didn't know what it meant. Once my friend's feet were "squeezed" we went to dinner.

The next day (Sunday) my mother called me around half past twelve in the afternoon. I picked up the phone and the first words out of her mouth were "I know what January third meant."

"What?" I asked.

She had just received a call from a relative that my cousin, Mark, was just found in his apartment "dead," and they were not sure when he "died". They weren't sure if it was January third or January fourth. That was what Nanny was talking about. The January third date was about my cousin Mark. He went to Heaven on the third. That is why the "family visit" happened the night before with me.

"It was for Mark", I shouted. His soul stayed by his bedside until his physical body was found. It was surely a sad experience all the way around, but I know he did have a peaceful transition.

During the days that followed, I tried as much as I could to be of help to his surviving brother, Brad who lives in Massachusetts with his wife in making the funeral arrangements. My cousin didn't know where to begin, being that he never had to plan a funeral. I met up with him at the funeral home and after several hours, the arrangements were made. Enter Nanny again. She told me to "Get the prayer cards".

Upon hearing this, I asked the funeral director if the ceremony my cousin decided on had, in fact, included the cards. His response was, "no".

It's a good thing Nanny was on top of things. We ordered the cards and the guest book. The funeral home helped my cousin write the obituary. I listened to the wording. It seemed fine. The date was not mentioned, but *all* the newspapers stated January Fourth. Can you believe after all that communication from Nanny about the date?

When people are on the verge of transitioning, and they say they are seeing and/or talking to angels or their relatives or friends in Heaven, they really are. Of course, it will look like a one-way conversation. For them, the veil between the Earth's dimension and Heaven is thinning, making it easier for them to see and hear all of them. I truly believe that people on the verge of transitioning are half in and half out of their bodies. They are making connections with those who are coming to get them and escort them into Heaven. Please don't think they are hallucinating or that it's the medication. Know their time is coming sooner rather than later and take comfort in knowing they will have a smooth transition and because God and his house named Heaven, are ready to welcome them home.

How does this all tie into this book? I want you to understand that we are never alone. Even when we transition alone, people on the other side (your pets, your angels, your guides, saints, Jesus, Buddha or whomever you believe in) are always there to pick us up and guide us into Heaven. Sometimes we think, *oh poor so and so, they were alone when they "died"*. Yes, it seems that way. While the person may not have been with anyone on this plane, he or she was greeted and guided into the gates of Heaven by everyone he or she knew and everyone the person believed in.

It's been shown to me so many times by folks that have transitioned that there is a huge reception, or homecoming celebration, to greet us when we arrive. The colors are beautiful and more striking than they are on this plane. There is no rain. No clouds. No pollution. No sickness. Heaven is a beautiful place. The food looks great too, and the flowers are magnificent. Everyone is happy, healthy and at peace. Oh, did I mention young too? Also, those in the afterlife can portray any look they wish.

So, this "Last Chapter" is almost like a first chapter. It depends on how we perceive life and life afterlife. Our soul always exists and never dies. Instead, we continually change form from one existence to another one.

Even though Heaven is a beautiful place, I am in no rush to be there. It is a blessing to be alive and experience this beautiful planet and all it has to offer. It is especially exciting to be alive at this time in history. Even though many personal challenges and planetary changes are taking place, human consciousness is shifting and evolving to be more aware of the here and now and the hereafter.

Isn't it comforting to know you are being watched over and being waited for by those you love and those who love you? I do.

Peace, love, and happiness,
Vanessa Lynn

Made in the USA
Middletown, DE
26 September 2018